ICE CREAM

ICE CREAM

AMAZING ICES, SHERBETS, SORBETS, BOMBES
AND ICED DESSERTS: 150 DELICIOUS RECIPES SHOWN
IN 300 BEAUTIFUL PHOTOGRAPHS

Joanna Farrow and Sara Lewis

LORENZ BOOKS

This edition is published by Lorenz Books,
an imprint of Anness Publishing Ltd,
Hermes House,
88–89 Blackfriars Road,
London SE1 8HA
tel. 020 7401 2077; fax 020 7633 9499

www.lorenzbooks.com; www.annesspublishing.com

If you like the images in this book and would like
to investigate using them for publishing, promotions
or advertising, please visit our website
www.practicalpictures.com for more information.

UK agent: The Manning Partnership Ltd;
tel. 01225 478444; fax 01225 478440;
sales@manning-partnership.co.uk
UK distributor: Grantham Book Services Ltd;
tel. 01476 541080; fax 01476 541061;
orders@gbs.tbs-ltd.co.uk
North American agent/distributor:
National Book Network; tel. 301 459 3366;
fax 301 429 5746; www.nbnbooks.com
Australian agent/distributor: Pan Macmillan Australia;
tel. 1300 135 113; fax 1300 135 103;
customer.service@macmillan.com.au
New Zealand agent/distributor: David Bateman Ltd;
tel. (09) 415 7664; fax (09) 415 8892

Publisher: Joanna Lorenz
Senior Managing Editor: Conor Kilgallon
Recipes: Joanna Farrow and Sara Lewis
Photography: Gus Filgate (recipes), Craig Robertson
(equipment and techniques, steps and still lifes).
Editor: Brian Burns
Designer: Nigel Partridge
Production Controller: Mai Ling Collyer

ETHICAL TRADING POLICY

At Anness Publishing we believe that business should
be conducted in an ethical and ecologically sustainable
way, with respect for the environment and a proper
regard to the replacement of the natural resources
we employ.

As a publisher, we use a lot of wood pulp to
make high-quality paper for printing, and that wood
commonly comes from spruce trees. We are therefore
currently growing more than 750,000 trees in three
Scottish forest plantations: Berrymoss (130 hectares/
320 acres), West Touxhill (125 hectares/305 acres) and
Deveron Forest (75 hectares/185 acres). The forests we
manage contain more than 3.5 times the number of
trees employed each year in making paper for the
books we manufacture.

Because of this ongoing ecological investment
programme, you, as our customer, can have the
pleasure and reassurance of knowing that a tree is
being cultivated on your behalf to naturally replace the
materials used to make the book you are holding.

Our forestry programme is run in accordance with
the UK Woodland Assurance Scheme (UKWAS) and
will be certified by the internationally recognized
Forest Stewardship Council (FSC). The FSC is a non-
government organization dedicated to promoting
responsible management of the world's forests.
Certification ensures forests are managed in an
environmentally sustainable and socially responsible
way. For further information about this scheme, go
to www.annesspublishing.com/trees

NOTES

For all recipes, quantities are given in both metric
and imperial measures and, where appropriate, in
standard cups and spoons.

Follow one set of measures, but not a
mixture, because they are not interchangeable.

Standard spoon and cup measures are level.
1 tsp = 5ml, 1 tbsp = 15ml, 1 cup = 250ml/8fl oz.

Australian standard tablespoons are 20ml.
Australian readers should use 3 tsp in place of
1 tbsp for measuring small quantities.

American pints are 16fl oz/2 cups. American
readers should use 20fl oz/2.5 cups in place of
1 pint when measuring liquids.

Electric oven temperatures in this book are
for conventional ovens. When using a fan oven,
the temperature will probably need to be
reduced by about 10–20°C/20–40°F. Since ovens
vary, you should check with your manufacturer's
instruction book for guidance.

The nutritional analysis given for each recipe
is calculated per portion (i.e. serving or item),
unless otherwise stated. If the recipe gives a
range, such as Serves 4–6, then the nutritional
analysis will be for the smaller portion size, i.e.
6 servings. Measurements for sodium do not
include salt added to taste.

Medium (US large) eggs are used unless
otherwise stated.

Front cover shows Iced Tiramisu – for recipe,
see page 36.

Recipes in this book previously appeared in
Ice Cream and Iced Desserts

Contents

The world of ice cream

Ice cream must be one of the few dishes that is loved by virtually everyone, from the very young to the out-and-out foodie. Whether your tastes are traditional or you're in search of the ultimate flavour combination, ice cream has something for everyone.

FOR YOUR PLEASURE

With ice cream, there really is something for everyone. On one hand, there's the irresistible ice cream cone. On the other, there's the elaborate layered mould, perfect for entertaining. In between come simple ice creams, refreshing fruit sorbets and snow-like granitas, ideal for serving between courses to cleanse the palate.

ALL THE BEST

Contained in this comprehensive guide are the very best ice creams, water ices, sorbets and granitas, from the stunningly simple to the impressively elaborate. You'll find all the classics together with adventurous mixtures that prove just how exciting ice creams can be. Some of the desserts are highly indulgent, but there are also delicious low-fat treats.

We take you on a cook's tour of specialities from all around the world, and unravel the differences between sherbet and water ice, sorbet and semi-freddo, gelato and granita, guiding you through a maze of ingredients, flavourings and techniques. With easy-to-follow instructions, even the most inexperienced cook can attempt every recipe with confidence.

SUCCESSFUL ICES

There are lots of helpful tips for successful ices with or without an ice cream maker, and advice on the best way to store iced desserts after you have made them. Throughout the book, detailed serving instructions give guidance on transforming simple scoops of ice cream or sorbet into desserts that would not look out of place in the smartest restaurant.

There are elaborate moulded desserts and terrines, extravagant bombes and mousses, and a wide selection of more sophisticated and elegant desserts. Iced gateaux, for instance, come in all sorts of shapes and guises. Fruit and nut, biscuit and meringue – the combinations are endless and the results outstanding.

LEFT: *White chocolate castles will add a stylish, regal touch to any dinner table.*

ABOVE: *For true enthusiasts, kulfi, the subtle Indian classic, is not to be missed.*

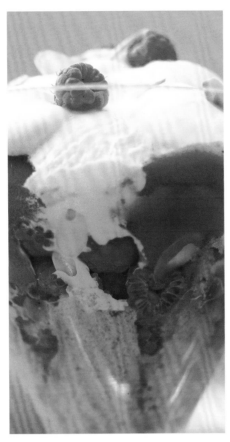

ABOVE: *Rich, yet cool, iced raspberry and almond trifle is an indulgent pleasure.*

ABOVE: *Enjoy a taste of the Middle East with saffron, apricot and almonds.*

Strawberry ice cream and lemon curd or rich chocolate ice cream and brownies complement each other perfectly. The more unusual iced brûlées, roulades or tortes look and taste superb, while ice cream sundaes get a modern makeover when layered in exquisite glasses with fruit and liqueur sauces. There is even a chapter that includes deliciously surprising hot ices.

AN INTERNATIONAL FLAVOUR

The range of recipes includes ice creams and water ices from the Mediterranean, Eastern Europe, India, the British Isles and the Americas. Some are sweetened with honey or maple syrup instead of sugar, while others are based upon yogurt or boiled milk, rather than cream. More unusual flavourings include flower essences, herbs (such as lavender and bay), nuts and spices.

AN AFFORDABLE TREAT

Ice cream is no longer considered a symbol of wealth, but is one of life's affordable luxuries. Universally acknowledged as one of the most popular comfort foods, it gives you a lift when you need it, and many problems have been solved – or friendships forged – over a tub of Chocolate Ripple or Rocky Road. So go on – enjoy it in all its glory.

ICE CREAM MAKERS

The recipes in this book give instructions for preparing and combining the ingredients by hand before freezing ("still freezing"). However, you can also use an ice cream maker to churn together the ingredients until firm enough to scoop or serve ("stir freezing"). For more detailed instructions on using ice cream makers, including advice on churning times and adding creams and additional flavourings such as nut praline, fruit purées and liqueurs, turn to pages 196 and 200–204.

Sorbets, sherbets, water ices & granitas

Nothing quite refreshes the palate as well as clean-tasting sorbets (also known as sherbets) or water ice. Stock up the freezer when fruits are plentiful to make effortless desserts throughout the year. Slushy granitas, with strong flavours such as ginger and tequila, are even easier to make.

Strawberry and lavender sorbet

Delicately perfumed with just a hint of lavender, this delightful pastel pink sorbet is perfect for a special-occasion dinner. If the lavender flowers are small, use as many as eight.

SERVES 6

150g/5oz/¾ cup caster
    (superfine) sugar
300ml/½ pint/1¼ cups water
6 fresh lavender flowers
500g/1¼lb/5 cups strawberries, hulled
1 egg white
lavender flowers, to decorate

1 Bring the sugar and water to the boil in a pan, stirring until the sugar has dissolved.

2 Take the pan off the heat, add the lavender flowers and infuse for 1 hour. Chill the syrup before using.

3 Purée the strawberries in a food processor. Press the purée through a large sieve (strainer) into a bowl.

4 Pour the purée into a plastic container, strain in the syrup and freeze for 4 hours until mushy. Then process in a food processor until smooth. Whisk the egg white until frothy, and stir into the sorbet. Spoon the sorbet back into the container and freeze until firm.

5 Serve in scoops, in tall glasses, and decorate with sprigs of lavender.

Nutritional information per portion: Energy 123kcal/523kJ; Protein 1.3g; Carbohydrate 31.1g, of which sugars 31.1g; Fat 0.1g, of which saturates 0g; Cholesterol 0mg; Calcium 27mg; Fibre 0.9g; Sodium 17mg.

Minted Earl Grey sorbet

Originally served in Georgian times at grand summer balls, this refreshing, slightly sharp sorbet is perfect for a lazy afternoon in the garden. It can be made as easily with tea bags as tea leaves.

SERVES 6

200g/7oz/1 cup caster (superfine) sugar
300ml/1/2 pint/11/4 cups water
1 lemon, well scrubbed
45ml/3 tbsp Earl Grey tea leaves
450ml/3/4 pint/2 cups boiling water
1 egg white
30ml/2 tbsp chopped fresh mint leaves
fresh mint sprigs or frosted mint,
   to decorate

1 In a pan, bring the caster sugar and water to the boil, stirring until the sugar has dissolved.

2 Thinly pare the rind from the lemon straight into the pan of syrup. Simmer for 2 minutes then pour into a bowl. Cool, then chill.

3 Put the tea into a pan and pour on the boiling water. Cover and leave to stand for 5 minutes, then strain into a bowl. Cool, then chill.

4 Pour the tea into a freezerproof container. Strain in the chilled syrup. Freeze for 4 hours.

5 Lightly whisk the egg white until just frothy. Scoop the sorbet into a food processor, process until smooth and mix in the mint and egg white. Spoon back into the tub and freeze for 4 hours until firm.

6 Serve in scoops, decorated with a few fresh or frosted mint leaves.

Nutritional information per portion: Energy 135kcal/578kJ; Protein 0.8g; Carbohydrate 35.1g, of which sugars 34.8g; Fat 0g, of which saturates 0g; Cholesterol 0mg; Calcium 29mg; Fibre 0g; Sodium 13mg.

Blackcurrant sorbet

Wonderfully sharp and bursting with flavour, this is a very popular sorbet. If you find it a bit sharp for your taste, add a little more sugar before freezing.

SERVES 6

500g/1¼lb/5 cups
   blackcurrants, trimmed
350ml/12fl oz/1½ cups water

150g/5oz/¾ cup caster (superfine) sugar
1 egg white
sprigs of blackcurrants, to decorate

1 Put the blackcurrants in a pan and add 150ml/¼ pint/⅔ cup of the measured water.

2 Cover the pan and simmer for 5 minutes or until the fruit is soft. Cool slightly, then purée in a food processor or blender.

3 Set a large sieve (strainer) over a bowl, pour the purée into the sieve then press it through the mesh with the back of a spoon.

4 Pour the remaining measured water into a clean pan. Add the sugar and bring to the boil, stirring until the sugar has dissolved. Pour the syrup into a bowl. Cool, then chill. Mix the blackcurrant purée and sugar syrup together.

5 Spoon into a plastic tub or similar freezerproof container and freeze for about 4 hours until mushy. Lightly whisk the egg white until just frothy. Spoon the sorbet into a food processor, process until smooth, then return it to the container and stir in the egg white. Freeze for 4 hours or until firm. Serve decorated with the blackcurrant sprigs.

VARIATION
This basic recipe can also be used to make raspberry sorbet. You will need 500g/1¼ lb/5 cups fresh raspberries. See also page 204 for more on making basic sorbets and berry purées.

Nutritional information per portion: Energy 84kcal/361kJ; Protein 1.3g; Carbohydrate 21.2g, of which sugars 21.2g; Fat 0g, of which saturates 0g; Cholesterol 0mg; Calcium 58mg; Fibre 3g; Sodium 14mg.

Lemon sorbet

Sorbets can be made from any citrus fruit but this is probably the all-time classic sorbet. Refreshingly tangy and yet deliciously smooth, it quite literally melts in the mouth.

SERVES 6

200g/7oz/1 cup caster (superfine) sugar
300ml/¹⁄₂ pint/1¹⁄₄ cups water
4 lemons, well scrubbed
1 egg white
sugared lemon rind, to decorate

1 Boil the sugar and water in a pan, stirring until the sugar dissolves. Thinly pare the rind of two lemons straight into the pan. Simmer for 2 minutes without stirring. Take the pan off the heat. Leave to cool, then chill. Add the juice from all the lemons to the syrup and strain into a shallow freezerproof container, reserving the rind. Freeze for 4 hours until mushy.

2 Beat in a food processor until smooth. Lightly whisk the egg white until it is just frothy. Spoon the sorbet back into the tub, beat in the egg white and freeze for 4 hours. Scoop into bowls or glasses and decorate with sugared lemon rind.

VARIATION
Sorbet can be made from any citrus fruit. Use 300ml/¹⁄₂ pint/1¹⁄₄ cups fresh fruit juice and the pared rind of half the squeezed fruits. Use 4 oranges or 2 oranges and 2 lemons, for orange sorbet. For lime sorbet, combine the rind of 3 limes with the juice of 6.

Nutritional information per portion: Energy 134kcal/571kJ; Protein 0.7g; Carbohydrate 35g, of which sugars 35g; Fat 0g, of which saturates 0g; Cholesterol 0mg; Calcium 19mg; Fibre 0g; Sodium 12mg.

Pear and Sauternes sorbet

Based on a traditional sorbet that would have been served between savoury courses, this fruity ice is delicately flavoured with the honeyed bouquet of Sauternes wine, spiked with brandy.

SERVES 6

675g/1½lb ripe pears
50g/2oz/¼ cup caster (superfine) sugar
250ml/8fl oz/1 cup water plus
   60ml/4 tbsp extra
250ml/8fl oz/1 cup Sauternes wine, plus
   extra to serve
30ml/2 tbsp brandy
juice of ½ lemon
1 egg white
fresh mint sprigs, dusted with icing
   (confectioners') sugar, to decorate

1 Quarter, peel and core the pears, and slice them into a pan. Add the sugar and 60ml/4 tbsp of water. Cover and simmer until the pears are just tender. Then blend in a food processor or blender until smooth. Scrape into a bowl. Leave to cool, then chill.

2 Stir the wine, brandy, lemon juice and remaining water into the purée.

3 Freeze in a freezerproof container for 4 hours, then beat in a food processor or blender until smooth. Return the sorbet to the tub.

4 Lightly whisk the egg white with a fork until just frothy and stir into the sorbet in the tub. Return to the freezer until the sorbet is firm enough to scoop. Serve the sorbet in small dessert glasses, with a little extra Sauternes poured over each portion. Decorate with the sugared mint sprigs.

Nutritional information per portion: Energy 130kcal/549kJ; Protein 1g; Carbohydrate 22.4g, of which sugars 22.4g; Fat 0.1g, of which saturates 0g; Cholesterol 0mg; Calcium 23mg; Fibre 2.5g; Sodium 20mg.

Red berry sorbet

This vibrant red sorbet seems to capture the true flavour of summer. Pick your own berries, if you can, and use them as soon as possible.

SERVES 6

150g/5oz/³/₄ cup caster (superfine) sugar
200ml/7fl oz/scant 1 cup water
500g/1¼lb/5 cups mixed ripe berries, hulled, including two or more of the following: strawberries, raspberries, tayberries or loganberries

juice of ¹/₂ lemon
1 egg white
small whole and halved strawberries and strawberry leaves and flowers, to decorate

1 Put the sugar and water into a pan and bring to the boil, stirring until the sugar has dissolved. Pour the syrup into a bowl, leave to cool, then chill.

2 Purée the fruits in a food processor or blender, then press through a sieve (strainer) into a large bowl. Stir in the syrup and lemon juice.

3 Pour the mixture into a plastic tub or similar freezerproof container and freeze for 4 hours until mushy. Transfer to a food processor, process until smooth, then return to the tub. Lightly whisk the egg white and stir into the mixture. Freeze for 4 hours.

4 Scoop on to plates or bowls, and decorate with fresh strawberries, leaves and flowers.

VARIATION
For a fruity sorbet with a hidden kick, add 45ml/3 tbsp vodka or cassis.
However, don't be too generous with the spirits or the sorbet will not freeze firm.

Nutritional information per portion: Energy 123kcal/523kJ; Protein 1.3g; Carbohydrate 31.1g, of which sugars 31.1g; Fat 0.1g, of which saturates 0g; Cholesterol 0mg; Calcium 27mg; Fibre 0.9g; Sodium 17mg.

Raspberry granita

Served solo, red granita is an excellent dessert for anyone on a fat-free diet. For something a little more indulgent, serve with whole berries and crème fraîche or clotted cream.

SERVES 6

115g/4oz/¹/₂ cup caster
    (superfine) sugar
300ml/¹/₂ pint/1¹/₄ cups water
500g/1¹/₄lb/3¹/₂ cups raspberries,
    hulled, plus extra to decorate
juice of 1 lemon
little sifted icing (confectioners')
    sugar, for dusting

1 Boil the sugar and water in a large pan, stirring until the sugar dissolves. Pour the sugar syrup into a bowl, leave to cool, then chill.

2 Purée the raspberries in a food processor/blender, then spoon into a fine sieve (strainer) over a bowl. Press the purée through the sieve with the back of the spoon. Discard the seeds.

3 Scrape the purée into a measuring jug, stir in the sugar syrup and lemon juice and top up to 1 litre/1³/₄ pints/4 cups with cold water.

4 Pour the mixture into a large plastic container so that the depth is no more than 2.5cm/1in. Cover and freeze for 2 hours until the mixture around the sides is mushy.

5 Using a fork, break up the ice crystals and mash finely. Return to the freezer for 2 hours, beating every 30 minutes until the ice forms fine, even crystals.

6 Spoon into tall glass dishes and decorate with extra raspberries, dusted with icing sugar.

Nutritional information per portion: Energy 96kcal/413kJ; Protein 1.3g; Carbohydrate 23.9g, of which sugars 23.9g; Fat 0.3g, of which saturates 0.1g; Cholesterol 0mg; Calcium 31mg; Fibre 2.1g; Sodium 4mg.

Tequila and orange granita

Full of flavour, this distinctive Mexican granita will have guests clamouring for more.
Serve simply with wedges of citrus fruit or spoon over a little grenadine.

SERVES 6

115g/4oz/¹/₂ cup caster
 (superfine) sugar
300ml/¹/₂ pint/1¹/₄ cups water
juice of 6 oranges, and the rinds of 3
90ml/6 tbsp tequila
orange and lime wedges to decorate

1 Put the sugar and water into a pan. Using a vegetable peeler, thinly pare the rind from three of the oranges, letting it fall into the pan. Bring to the boil, stirring to dissolve the sugar. Pour the syrup into a bowl. Cool, then chill.

2 Strain the syrup into a shallow plastic container. Strain the orange juice into the syrup. Stir in the tequila. The mixture should be no more than 2.5cm/1in deep; transfer to a larger container if needed.

3 Cover and freeze for 2 hours until the mixture around the sides of the container is mushy. Mash well with a fork and return the granita to the freezer.

4 Freeze for 2 hours more, mashing the mixture with a fork every 30 minutes until the granita has a fine slushy consistency.

5 Scoop the granita into dishes and serve with the orange and lime wedges.

Nutritional information per portion: Energy 146kcal/618kJ; Protein 1.2g; Carbohydrate 28.5g, of which sugars 28.5g; Fat 0.1g, of which saturates 0g; Cholesterol 0mg; Calcium 57mg; Fibre 1.7g; Sodium 6mg.

Ruby grapefruit granita

This is slightly sharper than the other granitas, but is very refreshing. It's the ideal choice for serving after a rich or very filling main course.

SERVES 6

200g/7oz/1 cup caster (superfine) sugar
300ml/½ pint/1¼ cups water
4 ruby (pink) grapefruit
tiny mint leaves, to decorate

1 Put the sugar and water into a pan. Bring the water to the boil, stirring until the sugar has dissolved. Pour the syrup into a bowl, cool, then chill.

2 Cut the grapefruit in half. Squeeze the juice, taking care not to damage the grapefruit shells. Set these aside. Strain the juice into a large plastic container. Stir in the chilled syrup, making sure that the depth of the mixture does not exceed 2.5cm/1in.

3 Cover and freeze for 2 hours or until the mixture around the sides of the container is mushy. Using a fork, break up the ice crystals and mash the granita finely.

4 Freeze for 2 hours more, mashing the mixture every 30 minutes until the granita consists of fine, even crystals.

5 Select the six best grapefruit shells for use as the serving dishes. Using a sharp knife, remove the grapefruit pulp, leaving the shells as clean as possible.

6 Scoop the granita into the grapefruit shells, decorate with the tiny mint leaves and serve.

Nutritional information per portion: Energy 163kcal/695kJ; Protein 1g; Carbohydrate 42.1g, of which sugars 42.1g; Fat 0.1g, of which saturates 0g; Cholesterol 0mg; Calcium 42mg; Fibre 1.4g; Sodium 5mg.

Ginger granita

This full-bodied granita is an absolute must for ginger lovers. Served solo, it is a simple and inexpensive yet smart dessert.

SERVES 6

150g/5oz/¾ cup caster (superfine) sugar
1 litre/1¾ pints/4 cups water
75g/3oz fresh root ginger
a little ground cinnamon, to decorate

1 Put the sugar and water into a pan. Bring to the boil, stirring until the sugar has dissolved. Then take the pan off the heat.

2 Peel the ginger, chop it finely, then stir it into the hot sugar syrup. Leave for at least 1 hour to infuse and cool, then pour into a bowl and chill.

3 Strain the chilled syrup into a large, shallow plastic container, making sure the depth is no more than 2.5cm/1in. Cover and freeze for 2 hours or until the mixture around the sides of the container has become mushy.

4 Using a fork, break up the ice crystals and mash finely. Return the granita to the freezer for 2 hours more, beating every 30 minutes until the ice becomes soft and very fine with evenly sized ice crystals.

5 After the final beating, return the now slushy granita to the freezer. Serve in tall glasses decorated with ground cinnamon.

Nutritional information per portion: Energy 99kcal/420kJ; Protein 0.1g; Carbohydrate 26.1g, of which sugars 26.1g; Fat 0g, of which saturates 0g; Cholesterol 0mg; Calcium 13mg; Fibre 0g; Sodium 2mg.

Apple and cider water ice

This pleasing combination has a subtle apple flavour with a hint of cider. As the apple purée is very pale, a few drops of green food colouring will echo the pale green skin of the eating apples.

SERVES 6

500g/1¼lb Granny Smith
  (eating) apples
150g/5oz/¾ cup caster
  (superfine) sugar
300ml/½ pint/1¼ cups water
250ml/8fl oz/1 cup strong dry cider
few drops of green food
  colouring (optional)
strips of thinly pared lime rind,
  to decorate

1 Quarter, core and roughly chop the apples. Put them into a pan. Add the caster sugar and half the water. Cover and simmer for 10 minutes or until the apples are soft.

2 Press the mixture through a sieve (strainer) placed over a bowl. Discard the apple skins and seeds. Stir the cider and the remaining water into the apple purée and add a little colouring, if you like.

3 Pour into a shallow plastic container and freeze for 6 hours, beating with a fork once or twice to break up the ice crystals.

4 Scoop into dishes and decorate with twists of thinly pared lime rind.

Nutritional information per portion: Energy 143kcal/610kJ; Protein 0.4g; Carbohydrate 34.6g, of which sugars 34.6g; Fat 0.1g, of which saturates 0g; Cholesterol 0mg; Calcium 20mg; Fibre 1.3g; Sodium 6mg.

Damson water ice

For this recipe, use ripe fruits for natural sweetness. If you can't find damsons, use another deep red variety of plum or extra-juicy Victoria plums. Apricot water ice can be made in the same way.

SERVES 6

500g/1¼lb ripe damsons, washed

450ml/¾ pint/scant 2 cups water

150g/5oz/⅔ cup caster
(superfine) sugar

1 Simmer the damsons and 150ml/¼ pint/⅔ cup of water in a covered pan until the damsons are tender.

2 In a second pan, boil the remaining water and sugar, stirring until the sugar dissolves. Pour the syrup into a bowl, leave to cool, then chill.

3 Mash the damsons with a wooden spoon, discarding loose stones. Strain the fruit and juices over a bowl, pressing with the back of a spoon. Discard the skins and any remaining stones.

4 Stir the syrup into the purée in a shallow plastic container and freeze for 6 hours, beating once or twice to break up the ice crystals.

5 Spoon into tall glasses or dishes and serve with wafer biscuits.

Nutritional information per portion: Energy 130kcal/555kJ; Protein 0.6g; Carbohydrate 34.1g, of which sugars 34.1g; Fat 0g, of which saturates 0g; Cholesterol 0mg; Calcium 33mg; Fibre 1.5g; Sodium 3mg.

Vanilla, chocolate & coffee ice creams

This chapter provides the best vanilla ice cream recipes, plus some imaginative variations using ingredients such as brandy, whisky, crumbled cookies, herb flowers and cinnamon. The flavours of chocolate, coffee and toffee ice cream are many people's favourites, making this selection the ultimate collection of classic ice creams.

Classic vanilla ice cream

Nothing beats the creamy simplicity of true vanilla ice cream. And once you've tried this luxurious home-made version, there's no going back.

SERVES 4

1 vanilla pod (bean)
300ml/½ pint/1¼ cups semi-skimmed (low-fat) milk
4 egg yolks
75g/3oz/6 tbsp caster (superfine) sugar
5ml/1 tsp cornflour (cornstarch)
300ml/½ pint/1¼ cups double (heavy) cream

1 Slit the vanilla pod lengthways. Pour the milk into a heavy pan, add the vanilla pod and bring to the boil. Remove from the heat and leave for 15 minutes.

2 Hold the pod over the pan and, with a small knife, scrape the seeds into the milk. Return the pan to the heat and bring back to the boil.

3 Whisk the egg yolks, sugar and cornflour in a bowl until thick and foamy. Gradually pour on the hot milk, whisking constantly. Return the mixture to the pan and cook over a gentle heat, stirring all the time.

4 When the custard thickens and is smooth, pour it back into the bowl. Cool it, then chill.

5 Whip the cream until it has thickened but still falls from a spoon. Fold it into the custard and pour into a plastic tub or similar freezerproof container.

6 Freeze for 6 hours or until firm enough to scoop, beating twice with a fork, or in a food processor.

7 Scoop into dishes, bowls or bought cones – or eat straight from the tub.

Nutritional information per portion: Energy 546kcal/2264kJ; Protein 6.8g; Carbohydrate 25.6g, of which sugars 24.4g; Fat 47.1g, of which saturates 27.4g; Cholesterol 309mg; Calcium 160mg; Fibre 0g; Sodium 60mg.

Brown bread ice cream

This classic ice cream is flecked with tiny clusters of crisp, crunchy, caramelized brown breadcrumbs and tastes like cookies-and-cream ice cream.

SERVES 4–6

4 egg yolks
75g/3oz/6 tbsp caster (superfine) sugar
5ml/1 tsp cornflour (cornstarch)
300ml/½ pint/1¼ cups semi-skimmed (low-fat) milk
40g/1½oz/3 tbsp butter
75g/3oz/1½ cups fresh brown breadcrumbs
50g/2oz/¼ cup soft light brown sugar
5ml/1 tsp natural vanilla extract
300ml/½ pint/1¼ cups double (heavy) cream

1 Whisk the egg yolks, sugar and cornflour in a bowl until thick and pale. Bring the milk to the boil in a heavy pan, then gradually pour it on to the egg yolk mixture, whisking constantly.

2 Return the mixture to the pan. Heat gently, stirring until thick. Pour back into the bowl, leave to cool, then chill.

3 Melt the butter in a frying pan. Add the breadcrumbs, stir until evenly coated in butter. Sprinkle the sugar over. Fry for 4–5 minutes, stirring until lightly browned. Remove from the heat and leave until cool and crisp.

4 Add the vanilla extract to the custard and mix well. Whip the cream until thick then fold into the custard. Transfer to a container. Freeze for 4 hours, beating once.

5 Break up the breadcrumbs with your fingers. Beat the ice cream briefly, then stir in the breadcrumbs. Return to the freezer until firm enough to scoop.

Nutritional information per portion: Energy 418kcal/1735kJ; Protein 4.2g; Carbohydrate 28g, of which sugars 17.2g; Fat 32.5g, of which saturates 19.2g; Cholesterol 125mg; Calcium 62mg; Fibre 0.3g; Sodium 144mg.

Gingered semi-freddo

This Italian ice cream is rather like the original soft-scoop ice cream. Made with a boiled sugar syrup rather than a traditional egg custard, and generously speckled with ginger, this delicious ice cream will stay soft when frozen.

SERVES 6

4 egg yolks
115g/4oz/generous ½ cup caster
 (superfine) sugar
120ml/4fl oz/½ cup cold water
300ml/½ pints/1¼ cups double
 (heavy) cream

115g/4oz/²/₃ cup drained preserved
 stem ginger, finely chopped, plus
 extra slices, to decorate
45ml/3 tbsp whisky (optional)

1 Put the egg yolks in a large heatproof bowl and whisk until frothy. Then bring a pan of water to the boil and simmer gently.

2 Mix the sugar and measured cold water in another pan and heat gently, stirring occasionally, until the sugar has dissolved.

3 Increase the heat and boil for 4–5 minutes without stirring, until the syrup registers 119°C/238°F on a sugar thermometer. Alternatively, test by dropping a little of the syrup into a cup of cold water. Pour the water away. You should be able to mould the syrup into a ball.

4 Put the bowl of egg yolks over the pan of simmering water and whisk in the sugar syrup. Continue whisking until the mixture is very thick. Remove from the heat and whisk until cool.

5 Whip the cream and lightly fold it into the yolk mixture, with the chopped ginger and whisky, if using. Pour into a plastic tub or similar freezerproof container and still freeze for 1 hour.

6 Stir the semi-freddo to bring any ginger that has sunk to the bottom of the tub to the top, then return to the freezer for 5–6 hours until firm. Scoop into dishes or chocolate cases. Decorate with slices of ginger.

Nutritional information per portion: Energy 371kcal/1539kJ; Protein 3g; Carbohydrate 22.4g, of which sugars 22.3g; Fat 30.6g, of which saturates 17.8g; Cholesterol 203mg; Calcium 55mg; Fibre 0.5g; Sodium 23mg.

Cookies and cream

This wickedly indulgent ice cream is a favourite in the USA. To make the result even more luxurious, use freshly baked home-made biscuits with large chunks of chocolate and nuts.

SERVES 4–6

4 egg yolks
75g/3oz/6 tbsp caster (superfine) sugar
5ml/1 tsp cornflour (cornstarch)
300ml/½ pint/1¼ cups semi-skimmed (low-fat) milk
5ml/1 tsp natural vanilla extract
300ml/½ pint/1¼ cups whipping cream
150g/5oz chunky chocolate and hazelnut biscuits, crumbled into chunky pieces

1 Whisk the egg yolks, sugar and cornflour in a bowl until thick and foamy. Bring the milk to the boil in a heavy pan. Pour it on to the egg yolk mixture, whisking constantly.

2 Return to the pan and cook gently, stirring until the custard is thick and smooth. Pour back into the bowl and cover closely. Leave to cool, then chill.

3 Stir the vanilla extract into the custard. Whip the cream until thickened but soft enough to fall from a spoon.

4 Fold the cream into the chilled custard, then pour into a freezerproof container. Freeze for 4 hours, beating once to break up the ice crystals. Beat one more time, then fold in the biscuit chunks. Cover and return to the freezer until firm.

Nutritional information per portion: Energy 428kcal/1782kJ; Protein 6.2g; Carbohydrate 36.3g, of which sugars 27.1g; Fat 29.7g, of which saturates 16.4g; Cholesterol 189mg; Calcium 135mg; Fibre 0.5g; Sodium 129mg.

Crème fraîche and honey ice

This delicately flavoured vanilla ice cream is delicious either served on its own or with slices of hot apple or cherry pie. Don't be too generous with the honey or it will dominate the dish.

SERVES 4

4 egg yolks
60ml/4 tbsp clear flower honey
5ml/1 tsp cornflour (cornstarch)
300ml/¹/₂ pint/1¹/₄ cups semi-skimmed (low-fat) milk
7.5ml/1¹/₂ tsp natural vanilla extract
250g/9oz/generous 1 cup crème fraîche
nasturtium, pansy or herb flowers, to decorate

1 Whisk the egg yolks, honey and cornflour in a bowl until thick and foamy. Pour the milk into a heavy pan, bring to the boil, then gradually pour on to the egg yolk mixture, whisking constantly.

2 Return the mixture to the pan and cook over a gentle heat, stirring all the time until the custard thickens and is smooth. Pour the thickened mixture back into the bowl, then chill.

3 Stir in the vanilla extract and crème fraîche. Then pour into a plastic tub or similar freezerproof container. Freeze for 6 hours or until firm enough to scoop, beating once or twice with a fork or in a food processor or blender to break up the ice crystals.

4 Serve in glass dishes and then decorate with nasturtiums, pansies or herb flowers.

Nutritional information per portion: Energy 386kcal/1602kJ; Protein 6.9g; Carbohydrate 16.5g, of which sugars 16.3g; Fat 33g, of which saturates 19.5g; Cholesterol 277mg; Calcium 151mg; Fibre 0g; Sodium 57mg.

Classic dark chocolate

Rich, dark and wonderfully luxurious, this ice cream can be served solo or drizzled with warm chocolate sauce. If you are making it in advance, don't forget to soften the ice cream before serving so that the full flavour of the chocolate comes through.

SERVES 4–6

4 egg yolks
75g/3oz/6 tbsp caster (superfine) sugar
5ml/1 tsp cornflour (cornstarch)
300ml/¹/₂ pint/1¹/₄ cups semi-skimmed
    (low-fat) milk

200g/7oz dark (bittersweet) chocolate
300ml/¹/₂ pint/1¹/₄ cups whipping cream
shaved chocolate, to decorate

1 Whisk the egg yolks, sugar and cornflour in a bowl until thick and foamy. Pour the milk into a pan, bring it just to the boil, then gradually whisk it into the egg yolk mixture.

2 Return the mixture to the pan and cook over a gentle heat, stirring constantly until the custard thickens and is smooth. Take the pan off the heat.

3 Break the chocolate into small pieces and stir into the hot custard until it has melted. Leave to cool, then chill.

4 Whip the cream until it has thickened but still falls from a spoon. Fold into the custard then pour into a plastic tub or similar freezerproof container. Freeze for 6 hours or until firm enough to scoop, beating once or twice with a fork or in a food processor.

5 Serve in scoops, decorated with chocolate shavings.

VARIATION
This basic recipe can also be used to make double white chocolate ice cream. However, you will need 200g/7oz white chocolate, chopped, and 10ml/2tsp natural vanilla extract, which you should add when you add the chocolate to the hot custard.

Nutritional information per portion: Energy 349kcal/1461kJ; Protein 4.8g; Carbohydrate 36.8g, of which sugars 35.8g; Fat 21.4g, of which saturates 11.9g; Cholesterol 162mg; Calcium 78mg; Fibre 0.7g; Sodium 29mg.

C 'n' C sherbet

This dark chocolate sherbet is a cross between a water ice and a light, cream-free ice cream, and is ideal for chocoholics who are eagerly trying to count calories.

SERVES 4–6

600ml/1 pint/2¹/₂ cups semi-skimmed
   (low-fat) milk
40g/1¹/₂oz/¹/₃ cup good quality
   unsweetened cocoa powder
115g/4oz/¹/₂ cup caster
   (superfine) sugar
5ml/1 tsp instant coffee granules
chocolate-covered raisins, to decorate

1 Heat the milk in a pan. Meanwhile, put the cocoa in a bowl. Add a little of the hot milk to the cocoa and mix to a paste.

2 Add the remaining milk to the cocoa mixture, stirring all the time, then pour the chocolate milk back into the pan. Bring to the boil, stirring constantly.

3 Take the pan off the heat and stir in the sugar and the coffee. Pour into a jug, leave to cool, then chill.

4 Pour the mixture into a plastic tub and freeze for 6 hours until firm, beating once or twice with a fork, blender or in a food processor to break up the ice crystals. Allow to soften slightly before serving.

Nutritional information per portion: Energy 142kcal/604kJ; Protein 4.7g; Carbohydrate 25.5g, of which sugars 24.7g; Fat 3.2g, of which saturates 1.9g; Cholesterol 6mg; Calcium 139mg; Fibre 0.8g; Sodium 108mg.

Dark chocolate and hazelnut praline ice cream

For nut lovers and chocoholics everywhere, this is the ultimate indulgence. If you fancy a change, you might like to try using other types of nuts for the praline instead.

SERVES 4–6

4 egg yolks

5ml/1 tsp cornflour (cornstarch)

175g/6oz/scant 1 cup granulated (white) sugar

300ml/½ pint/1¼ cups semi-skimmed (low-fat) milk

150g/5oz dark (bittersweet) chocolate, broken into squares

115g/4oz/1 cup hazelnuts

60ml/4 tbsp water

300ml/½ pint/1¼ cups whipping cream

1 Whisk the egg yolks, cornflour and half the sugar until thick and foamy. Bring the milk to the boil in a heavy pan, then pour it on to the yolk mixture, whisking constantly. Scrape back into the pan and cook gently, stirring until thick and smooth.

2 Take the pan off the heat and stir in the chocolate a few squares at a time. Cool, then chill. Brush a baking sheet with oil and set it aside.

3 Put the hazelnuts, remaining sugar and measured water in a large, heavy frying pan. Heat gently, without stirring until the sugar dissolves.

4 Increase the heat slightly and cook until the syrup turns pale golden. Quickly pour the mixture on to the oiled baking sheet and leave until the praline cools and hardens.

5 Whip the cream until thick but still soft enough to fall from a spoon. Fold it into the custard and freeze in a tub for 4 hours, beating once with a fork or electric whisk.

6 Break the praline into pieces. Reserve a few for decoration and finely chop the rest. Beat once more, then fold in the chopped praline. Freeze until firm.

Nutritional information per portion: Energy 624kcal/2602kJ; Protein 8.7g; Carbohydrate 52g, of which sugars 50.6g; Fat 43.8g, of which saturates 19.3g; Cholesterol 191mg; Calcium 155mg; Fibre 1.9g; Sodium 45mg.

Iced tiramisu

This favourite Italian combination is not usually served frozen, but it does make a marvellous ice cream. Like the more traditional version, it tastes deliciously rich.

SERVES 4

150g/5oz/³/₄ cup caster
   (superfine) sugar
150ml/¹/₄ pint/²/₃ cup water
250g/9oz/generous 1 cup mascarpone
200g/7oz/scant 1 cup virtually fat-free
   fromage frais (low-fat cream cheese)
5ml/1 tsp natural vanilla extract
10ml/2 tsp instant coffee, dissolved in
   30ml/2 tbsp boiling water
30ml/2 tbsp coffee liqueur or brandy
75g/3oz sponge finger biscuits
unsweetened cocoa powder, for dusting
chocolate curls, to decorate

1 Put 115g/4oz/¹/₂ cup of the sugar into a small pan. Add the water and bring to the boil, stirring until the sugar has dissolved. Leave the syrup to cool, then chill it.

2 Put the mascarpone into a bowl. Beat with a spoon until soft, then stir in the fromage frais. Add the chilled sugar syrup, a little at a time, then stir in the vanilla extract.

3 Spoon the mixture into a freezer-proof container and freeze for 4 hours, beating once to break up the ice crystals.

4 Put the coffee mixture in a small bowl, sweeten with the remaining sugar, add the liqueur or brandy, then stir well and leave to cool.

5 Finely crumble the biscuits and add to the coffee mixture. Then beat the ice cream again.

6 Spoon a third of the ice cream into a 900ml/1¹/₂ pint/3³/₄ cup plastic container, spoon over half the soaked biscuits, then top with half the remaining ice cream.

7 Sprinkle over the last of the coffee-soaked biscuits, then cover with the remaining ice cream. Freeze for 2–3 hours until firm enough to scoop. Dust with unsweetened cocoa powder and spoon into glass dishes. Decorate with chocolate curls, and serve.

Nutritional information per portion: Energy 362kcal/1526kJ; Protein 11.7g; Carbohydrate 54.5g, of which sugars 50.3g; Fat 10.5g, of which saturates 6.1g; Cholesterol 69mg; Calcium 78mg; Fibre 0.2g; Sodium 35mg.

Chunky chocolate ice cream

The three different chocolates in this decadent ice cream make it so delectable that it will rapidly disappear unless you hide it at the back of the freezer.

SERVES 4–6

4 egg yolks
75g/3oz/6 tbsp caster (superfine) sugar
5ml/1 tsp cornflour (cornstarch)
300ml/½ pint/1¼ cups semi-skimmed (low-fat) milk
200g/7oz milk chocolate
50g/2oz dark (bittersweet) chocolate, plus extra, to decorate
50g/2oz white chocolate
300ml/½ pint/1¼ cups whipping cream

1 Whisk the egg yolks, caster sugar and cornflour in a bowl until thick and foamy. In a heavy pan, bring the milk just to the boil, then gradually pour it on to the egg yolk mixture, whisking constantly.

2 Return the mixture to the pan and cook gently, stirring with a wooden spoon until thick and smooth.

3 Pour the custard back into the bowl. Break 150g|5oz of the milk chocolate into squares, stir these into the hot custard, then cover closely. Leave to cool, then chill. Chop the remaining milk, dark and white chocolate finely, and reserve to use later.

4 Whip the cream until thickened but soft enough to fall from a spoon. Fold into the custard and pour into a tub. Freeze for 4 hours, beating once with a fork or electric whisk.

5 Beat the ice cream one more time. Fold in the pieces of chocolate and freeze for 2–3 hours, or until firm enough to scoop. Decorate with pieces of dark chocolate.

Nutritional information per portion: Energy 564kcal/2352kJ; Protein 7.9g; Carbohydrate 47.7g, of which sugars 47.5g; Fat 39.3g, of which saturates 23g; Cholesterol 197mg; Calcium 175mg; Fibre 0.8g; Sodium 64mg.

Coffee frappé

This creamy, smooth creation for adults makes a wonderful alternative to a dessert on a hot summer's evening. Use cappuccino cups or small glasses for serving and provide your guests with straws and long-handled spoons.

SERVES 4

8 scoops of Classic Coffee ice cream
90ml/6 tbsp Kahlúa or Tia Maria liqueur
150ml/¼ pint/⅔ cup single (light) cream
1.5ml/¼ tsp ground cinnamon (optional)
crushed ice
ground cinnamon, for sprinkling

1 Put half the coffee ice cream in a food processor or blender. Add the liqueur, then pour in the cream, with a little cinnamon, if you like. (For a non-alcoholic version, use strong black coffee, instead of a liqueur.) Scoop the remaining ice cream into four cups or glasses.

2 Spoon the coffee cream mixture over the ice cream, then top with the crushed ice. Sprinkle with cinnamon and then serve immediately.

Nutritional information per portion: Energy 489kcal/2049kJ; Protein 8.2g; Carbohydrate 57.6g, of which sugars 55.6g; Fat 23.2g, of which saturates 15g; Cholesterol 73mg; Calcium 255mg; Fibre 0g; Sodium 136mg.

Warm chocolate float

Hot chocolate milkshake and scoops of chocolate and vanilla ice cream are combined here to make a meltingly delicious drink that will prove a big success with children and adults alike.

SERVES 2

115g/4oz plain (semisweet) chocolate, broken into pieces
250ml/8fl oz/1 cup milk
15ml/1 tbsp caster (superfine) sugar
4 large scoops of Classic Vanilla ice cream
4 large scoops of Classic Dark Chocolate ice cream
a little lightly whipped cream
grated chocolate or chocolate curls, to decorate

1 Put the chocolate in a pan and add the milk and sugar. Heat gently, stirring with a wooden spoon until the chocolate has melted and the mixture is smooth.

2 Place two scoops of each type of ice cream alternately in two heatproof tumblers.

3 Pour the chocolate milk over and around the ice cream. Top with lightly whipped cream and grated chocolate or chocolate curls.

Nutritional information per portion: Energy 918kcal/3834kJ; Protein 16.9g; Carbohydrate 92.2g, of which sugars 91.5g; Fat 56g, of which saturates 33.7g; Cholesterol 11mg; Calcium 423mg; Fibre 1.5g; Sodium 208mg.

Classic coffee ice cream

This bittersweet blend is a must for those who like their coffee strong and dark with just a hint of cream. When serving, decorate with the chocolate-covered coffee beans.

SERVES 4–6

90ml/6 tbsp fine filter coffee
250ml/8fl oz/1 cup boiling water
4 egg yolks
75g/3oz/6 tbsp caster (superfine) sugar
5ml/1 tsp cornflour (cornstarch)
300ml/½ pint/1¼ cups semi-skimmed (low-fat) milk
150ml/¼ pint/⅔ cup double (heavy) cream
chocolate-covered coffee beans, to decorate

1 Put the coffee in a cafetière or jug and pour on the boiling water. Leave to cool, then strain. Chill until needed.

2 Whisk the egg yolks, caster sugar and cornflour until thick and foamy. Bring the milk to the boil in a heavy pan, then slowly pour on to the yolk mixture, whisking constantly.

3 Return the mixture to the pan, stirring constantly and cooking gently until thick and smooth. Pour back into the bowl and cover with clear film. Cool, then chill.

4 Whip the cream until it has thickened but still falls from a spoon.

5 Fold into the custard, add the coffee, then pour into a plastic tub or similar freezerproof container. Freeze for 6 hours until firm, beating once or twice with a fork, electric mixer or in a food processor to break up the crystals.

6 Finally, serve in glass dishes and sprinkle with chocolate-covered coffee beans.

Nutritional information per portion: Energy 260kcal/1076kJ; Protein 2.6g; Carbohydrate 12.9g, of which sugars 10.2g; Fat 21.5g, of which saturates 12.5g; Cholesterol 53mg; Calcium 87mg; Fibre 0.1g; Sodium 39mg.

Coffee toffee swirl

A wonderful combination of creamy vanilla, marbled with coffee-flavoured toffee. Serve on its own or as a sundae with Classic Coffee and Chocolate ice cream.

SERVES 4–6

FOR THE TOFFEE SAUCE
10ml/2 tsp cornflour (cornstarch)
170g/5 3/4 oz can evaporated
   (unsweetened condensed) milk
75g/3oz/6 tbsp muscovado
   (molasses) sugar
20ml/4 tsp instant coffee granules
15ml/1tbsp boiling water

FOR THE ICE CREAM
4 egg yolks
75g/3oz/6 tbsp caster (superfine) sugar
5ml/1 tsp cornflour (cornstarch)
300ml/1/2 pint/1 1/4 cups semi-skimmed
   (low-fat) milk
5ml/1tsp vanilla extract
300ml/1/2 pint/1 1/4 cups whipping cream

1 In a small, heavy pan, mix cornflour and a little evaporated milk to a smooth paste. Add the sugar and remaining evaporated milk. Cook gently, stirring until the sugar dissolves, then increase the heat and cook, stirring constantly, until slightly thickened and darkening in colour.

2 Take off the heat. Mix the coffee with the boiling water and stir into the sauce. Cool by plunging the base of the pan into cold water.

3 Whisk the egg yolks, sugar and cornflour together until thick and foaming. Bring the milk just to the boil in a heavy pan and gradually whisk into the yolk mixture. Return to the pan and cook gently, stirring constantly until thickened and smooth. Pour back into the bowl, stir in the vanilla and leave to cool.

4 Whip the cream until thickened but soft enough to fall from a spoon. Fold into the custard, then freeze in a container for 4 hours, beating twice.

5 Beat the toffee sauce well and drizzle it over the ice cream. Marble together by roughly running a knife through the mixture. Cover and freeze the ice cream for 4-5 hours until it is firm enough to scoop.

Nutritional information per portion: Energy 580kcal/2432kJ; Protein 24.5g; Carbohydrate 46.3g, of which sugars 44g; Fat 34.6g, of which saturates 20.4g; Cholesterol 225mg; Calcium 805mg; Fibre 0g; Sodium 297mg.

Fruit & nut
ice creams

From classic fruit-flavoured ice creams to

those speckled with chopped toasted nuts,

this chapter imaginatively introduces the

most widely used ice cream flavours.

Fresh fruit purées, liqueured dried fruits

and crunchy nuts transform a basic

ice cream into something very special.

Passion fruit mousses

Passion fruit has an exotic, tangy flavour that works wonderfully well in a creamy mousse. Peel away the raised paper collar and the texture and sophisticated shape are revealed.

SERVES 6

9 ripe passion fruit
10ml/2 tsp powdered gelatine
45ml/3 tbsp water
3 eggs, separated

75g/3oz/6 tbsp caster (superfine) sugar
30ml/2 tbsp lemon juice
250ml/8fl oz/1 cup double (heavy)
    or whipping cream

1 First, make the paper collars. Cut out six 30 x 7.5cm/12 x 3in strips of baking parchment. Wrap each strip around a 150ml/¼ pint/⅔ cup ramekin, holding it in place with a paper clip. Secure with string under the rim of each paper collar.

2 Cut the passion fruit in half and use a teaspoon to scoop the pulp into a sieve (strainer) set over a bowl. Strain the pulp in the sieve, pressing with the back of a large spoon to extract as much juice as possible.

3 Sprinkle the gelatine over the water in a small, heatproof bowl and leave to soak for 5 minutes or until spongy. Whisk the egg yolks and sugar in a bowl until the mixture is pale and creamy.

4 Stand the bowl of gelatine in a pan with a little gently simmering water and leave until dissolved. Beat the passion fruit juice and lemon juice into the whisked mixture, then add the gelatine. Mix well. Leave to stand until thickened but not set. Whisk the egg whites until stiff. Whip the cream into soft peaks.

5 Using a large metal spoon, fold the cream into the yolk mixture. Stir in a quarter of the egg whites to loosen the mixture, then fold in the remainder. Spoon into the prepared dishes so that the mixture comes well above the rim of each dish. Freeze the mousses for at least 4 hours.

6 About 30 minutes before you intend to serve them, gently peel away the paper collars from the mousses and transfer them to the fridge to soften slightly.

Nutritional information per portion: Energy 585kcal/2414kJ; Protein 7.2g; Carbohydrate 8.5g, of which sugars 8.5g; Fat 58.4g, of which saturates 34.7g; Cholesterol 296mg; Calcium 77mg; Fibre 0.5g; Sodium 84mg.

Iced summer pudding

This frozen version of the classic soft-fruit dessert uses good-quality fruit sorbet and strawberry or raspberry ice cream. The result tastes just as delicious as it looks.

SERVES 6–8

25g/1 oz/2 tbsp caster (superfine) sugar
60ml/4 tbsp water
75ml/5 tbsp strawberry jam
60ml/4 tbsp crème de cassis
225g/8oz/2 cups small strawberries, thinly sliced

250g/9oz good quality Madeira cake
250ml/8fl oz/1 cup soft fruit sorbet
500ml/17fl oz/2¼ cups Simple Strawberry
  ice cream

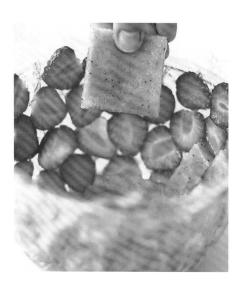

1 Line a 1.5 litre/2½ pint/6¼ cup bowl with clear film (plastic wrap). Heat the sugar and water in a small, heavy pan until the sugar has dissolved.

2 Press 30ml/2 tbsp of the strawberry jam through a sieve (strainer) into a small bowl. Stir in 15ml/1 tbsp of the syrup and brush the mixture up the sides of the lined bowl. Press the remaining jam through the sieve into the pan of syrup and stir in the crème de cassis until it is smooth.

3 Press the strawberry slices in a single layer over the base and sides of the lined bowl, fitting tightly together. Chill. Cut the cake into 1cm/½ in slices.

4 Dip the cake slices in the remaining syrup and arrange in a single layer over the strawberries, cutting the sponge to fit and trimming off the excess around the edges. Freeze for 30 minutes.

5 Remove the sorbet from the freezer to soften for about 15 minutes. Using a large metal spoon, pack the sorbet into the bowl – about three-quarters full – and level the surface. Return the bowl to the freezer for 30 minutes. Remove the ice cream from the freezer for about 15 minutes to soften.

6 Pack the ice cream over the sorbet, filling the bowl. Level the surface and freeze for at least 4 hours or overnight.

7 To serve, dip the bowl in very hot water for 2 seconds then invert the pudding on to a plate.

Nutritional information per portion: Energy 347kcal/1454kJ; Protein 4.5g; Carbohydrate 50.4g, of which sugars 43g; Fat 14.3g, of which saturates 8.3g; Cholesterol 0mg; Calcium 86mg; Fibre 0.6g; Sodium 165mg.

Lemon sorbet cups with summer fruits

In this stunning dessert, lemon sorbet is moulded into pretty containers for a selection of summer fruits. Other combinations such as mango and tropical fruits work just as well.

SERVES 6

500ml/17fl oz/2¼ cups Lemon Sorbet
225g/8oz/2 cups small strawberries
150g/5oz/scant 1 cup raspberries
75g/3oz/³⁄₄ cup redcurrants,
**   blackcurrants or whitecurrants**
15ml/1 tbsp caster (superfine) sugar
45ml/3 tbsp Cointreau or other
**   orange-flavoured liqueur**

1 Put six 150ml/¼ pint/²⁄₃ cup metal moulds in the freezer for 15 minutes to chill. At the same time, remove the sorbet from the freezer to soften slightly.

2 Using a teaspoon, pack the sorbet into the moulds, building up a layer about 1cm/½in thick around the base and sides, and leaving a deep cavity in the centre. Hold each mould in a dish towel as you work. Return each mould to the freezer when it is lined.

3 Cut the strawberries in half and place in a bowl with the raspberries and red-, black- or whitecurrants. Add the sugar and liqueur and toss the ingredients together lightly. Cover and chill for at least 2 hours.

4 Once the sorbet in the moulds has frozen completely, loosen the edges with a knife, then dip in a bowl of very hot water for 2 seconds. Invert the sorbet cups on a small tray, using a fork to twist and loosen the cups if necessary.

5 If you need to, dip the moulds very briefly in the hot water again. Turn the cups over so they are ready to fill and return to the freezer until required.

6 To serve, place the cups on serving plates and fill with the fruits, spooning over any juices.

Nutritional information per portion: Energy 159kcal/ 678kJ; Protein 1.4g; Carbohydrate 38.1g, of which sugars 38.1g; Fat 0.1g, of which saturates 0g; Cholesterol 0mg; Calcium 15mg; Fibre 0.8g; Sodium 21mg.

Spiced sorbet pears

Pears poached in wine make an elegant dessert at any time of the year. In this recipe, the pears are hollowed out and filled with a wine-and-pear flavoured sorbet.

SERVES 6

600ml/1 pint/2¹/₂ cups red wine
2 cinnamon sticks, halved
115g/4oz/generous ¹/₂ cup caster
   (superfine) sugar
6 plump pears

1 Gently heat the wine, cinnamon sticks and sugar in a large heavy pan, until the sugar dissolves.

2 Peel the pears, leaving the stalks attached. Stand them upright in the syrup in the pan, taking care not to pack them too tightly.

3 Cover and simmer very gently for 10–20 minutes until just tender, turning so they colour evenly.

4 Lift out the pears with a slotted spoon and set aside to cool. Briefly boil the juices to reduce to 350ml/ 12fl oz/1¹/₂ cups. Set aside to cool.

5 Cut a deep 2.5cm/1in slice off the top of each pear and reserve. Use an apple corer to remove the cores.

6 Using a teaspoon, scoop out the centre of each pear, leaving a thick shell. Put the scooped-out flesh in a food processor or blender, and the hollowed pears and their lids in the freezer. Strain the poaching juices.

7 Set 75ml/5 tbsp aside for serving and add the rest to the food processor. Blend until smooth.

8 Pour the mixture into a container and freeze for 3-4 hours, beating twice as it thickens. Using a teaspoon, pack the sorbet into the frozen pears, piling it up high. Position the lids and return to the freezer overnight.

9 Remove the pears from the freezer and stand at room temperature for 30 minutes before serving. Transfer to serving plates and spoon a little of the reserved syrup around each one.

Nutritional information per portion: Energy 198kcal/ 835kJ; Protein 0.6g; Carbohydrate 35.2g, of which sugars 35.2g; Fat 0.2g, of which saturates 0g; Cholesterol 0mg; Calcium 33mg; Fibre 3.3g; Sodium 12mg.

Marinated fruits with sorbet sauce

Whizzed briefly in the food processor with fruit juice and liqueur, sorbet makes a wonderful sauce for spooning over fruit.

SERVES 4

12 lychees, peeled
1 mango, peeled
1 papaya, peeled
1 kiwi fruit, peeled
juice of 1 lime
15ml/1 tbsp caster (superfine) sugar
60ml/4 tbsp vodka
300ml/½ pint/1¼ cups mango or other tropical fruit sorbet
30ml/2 tbsp mango or orange juice

1 Halve the lychees and remove the stones (pits). Then stone and slice the mango. Halve the papaya, remove the seeds and thinly slice or chop the flesh. Slice the kiwi fruit.

2 Put the fruits in a bowl. Add the lime juice, sugar and 15ml/1 tbsp of the vodka and toss together lightly with a spoon. Cover and chill for at least 1 hour.

3 Stir the fruits together lightly and divide among four tall, narrow glasses. Chill until ready to serve.

4 Scoop the sorbet into a food processor, then add the mango or orange juice and remaining vodka and blend very briefly until smooth and foamy. Immediately pour over the fruits and serve.

Nutritional information per portion: Energy 210kcal/886kJ; Protein 1.5g; Carbohydrate 47g, of which sugars 45.1g; Fat 0.4g, of which saturates 0g; Cholesterol 0mg; Calcium 39mg; Fibre 2.5g; Sodium 14mg.

Mascarpone and raspberry ripple

Mascarpone makes a refreshing base for ice cream, especially when mixed with lemon syrup and streaked with raspberry purée.

SERVES 8

250g/9oz/1¼ cups caster (superfine) sugar
450ml/¾ pint/scant 2 cups water
finely grated rind and juice of 1 lemon
350g/12oz/2 cups raspberries, plus extra, to decorate
500g/1¼lb/2½ cups mascarpone

1 Put 225g/8oz/1 cup of the sugar in a heavy pan. Pour in the water and heat gently until the sugar completely dissolves. Bring to the boil, add the lemon rind and juice and boil for 3 minutes, without stirring, to make a syrup. Leave to cool.

2 Crush the raspberries lightly with a fork until broken but not puréed. Stir in the remaining sugar.

3 Beat the mascarpone in a large bowl until smooth, gradually adding the lemon syrup.

4 Pour the mascarpone mixture into a freezer container and freeze for 3-4 hours, beating twice with a fork as it thickens.

5 Spoon the crushed raspberries over the ice cream. With a metal spoon, fold into the ice cream until rippled. Freeze overnight or until firm.

6 Decorate with raspberries and serve in glasses.

Nutritional information per portion: Energy 217kcal/916kJ; Protein 10.1g; Carbohydrate 36.9g, of which sugars 36.9g; Fat 5.1g, of which saturates 3.3g; Cholesterol 15mg; Calcium 100mg; Fibre 1.1g; Sodium 277mg.

Tutti frutti

This ice cream takes its name from an Italian expression meaning "all the fruits". Four fruits have been used here, but you can improvise to include exotics such as papaya or mango.

SERVES 4–6

300ml/¹/₂ pint/1¹/₄ cups semi-skimmed
   (low-fat) milk
1 vanilla pod (bean)
4 egg yolks
75g/3oz/6 tbsp caster (superfine) sugar
5ml/1 tsp cornflour (cornstarch)
300ml/¹/₂ pint/1¹/₄ cups whipping cream
150g/5oz/²/₃ cup multi-coloured glacé
   (candied) cherries
50g/2oz/¹/₃ cup sliced candied lime and
   orange peel
50g/2oz/¹/₃ cup candied pineapple

1 Slit the vanilla pod lengthways and bring to the boil with the milk in a heavy pan. Immediately remove from the heat and allow the flavour to infuse for 15 minutes.

2 With a narrow-bladed knife, scrape the small black seeds from the vanilla pod into the milk. Set the pod aside for later re-use. Gently bring the flavoured milk back to the boil.

3 Whisk the egg yolks, sugar and cornflour in a bowl until thick and foamy. Gradually whisk in the flavoured milk.

4 Pour the milk mixture back into the pan. Cook gently, stirring until thickened. Pour it back into the bowl and cover. Cool, then chill.

5 Whip the cream until thickened but soft enough to fall from a spoon. Then fold it into the custard.

6 Freeze the mixture in a freezerproof container for 4 hours, beating once with a fork or electric mixer.

7 Finely chop the glacé cherries, candied peel and pineapple, and fold into the ice cream. Then return to the freezer for 2–3 hours until firm enough to scoop.

Nutritional information per portion: Energy 405kcal/1694kJ; Protein 4.8g; Carbohydrate 44g, of which sugars 43.2g; Fat 24.6g, of which saturates 14.1g; Cholesterol 182mg; Calcium 146mg; Fibre 1g; Sodium 94mg.

Brandied fruit and rice ice cream

Based on a favourite Victorian rice ice cream, this rich dessert combines spicy rice pudding with a creamy egg custard flecked with brandy-soaked fruits.

SERVES 4–6

50g/2oz/¹⁄₃ cup ready-to-eat, pitted prunes, finely chopped

50g/2oz/¹⁄₃ cup ready-to-eat dried apricots, finely chopped

50g/2oz/¹⁄₄ cup glacé (candied) cherries, finely chopped

30ml/2 tbsp brandy

150ml/¹⁄₄ pint/²⁄₃ cup single (light) cream

FOR THE RICE MIXTURE

40g/1¹⁄₂oz/generous ¹⁄₄ cup pudding rice

450ml/³⁄₄ pint/scant 2 cups full-cream (whole) milk

1 cinnamon stick, halved, plus extra cinnamon sticks, to decorate

4 cloves

FOR THE CUSTARD

4 egg yolks

75g/3oz/6 tbsp caster (superfine) sugar

5ml/1 tsp cornflour (cornstarch)

300ml/¹⁄₂ pint/1¹⁄₄ cups full-cream (whole) milk

1 Put the chopped prunes, apricots and glacé cherries in a bowl. Pour over the brandy. Cover and leave to soak for 3 hours or overnight.

2 In a pan, bring the rice, milk and whole spices to the boil and simmer gently for 30 minutes, stirring occasionally until most of the milk has been absorbed. Lift out the spices and leave the rice to cool.

3 Whisk the egg yolks, sugar and cornflour in a bowl until thick and foamy. Heat the milk in a heavy pan, then gradually pour it on to the yolks, whisking constantly. Pour back into the pan and cook, stirring until the custard thickens. Leave to cool, then chill.

4 Mix the chilled custard, rice and cream together. Freeze for 4–5 hours until mushy, then beat with a fork to break up the ice crystals.

5 Fold in the fruits then freeze for 2–3 hours until firm enough to scoop. Serve with cinnamon sticks.

Nutritional information per portion: Energy 293kcal/1228kJ; Protein 8g; Carbohydrate 36.7g, of which sugars 30.7g; Fat 13.4g, of which saturates 7.2g; Cholesterol 166mg; Calcium 207mg; Fibre 1.1g; Sodium 73mg.

Peach and almond granita

Infused almonds make a richly flavoured "milk" that forms the basis of this light, tangy dessert, which would be the ideal choice to follow a rich main course.

SERVES 6

115g/4oz/1 cup ground almonds
900ml/1½ pints/3¾ cups water
150g/5oz/¾ cup caster (superfine) sugar
5ml/1 tsp almond extract

juice of 2 lemons
6 peaches
Disaronno Amaretto liqueur,
　to serve (optional)

1 Put the ground almonds in a pan and pour in 600ml/1 pint/2½ cups of the water. Bring just to the boil then lower the heat and simmer gently for 2 minutes. Remove from the heat and leave to stand for 30 minutes.

2 Strain the mixture through a fine sieve (strainer) placed over a bowl, and press lightly, with the back of a spoon, to extract as much liquid as possible. Pour the liquid into a clean, heavy pan.

3 Add the caster sugar and almond extract to the pan, with half the lemon juice and the remaining water. Heat gently until the sugar dissolves, then bring to the boil. Lower the heat and simmer gently for 3 minutes without stirring, taking care that the almond syrup does not boil over. Then leave to cool completely.

4 Cut the peaches in half and remove the stones (pits). Using a small knife, scoop out about half the flesh to enlarge the cavities. Put the flesh in a food processor. Brush the exposed flesh with the remaining lemon juice and chill the peaches until required.

5 Add the almond syrup to the peach flesh and process until smooth. Pour into a shallow freezer container and freeze until ice crystals have formed around the edges. Stir with a fork, then freeze again until more crystals have formed around the edges. Repeat until the mixture has the consistency of crushed ice.

6 Lightly break up the granita with a fork to loosen the mixture. Spoon into the peach halves and serve two on each plate. Drizzle a little Amaretto liqueur over the top, if you like.

Nutritional information per portion: Energy 239kcal/1005kJ; Protein 4.9g; Carbohydrate 32.8g, of which sugars 32.3g; Fat 10.8g, of which saturates 0.9g; Cholesterol 0mg; Calcium 64mg; Fibre 2.5g; Sodium 5mg.

Strawberry semi-freddo

Serve this quick strawberry and ricotta dessert semi-frozen to enjoy the flavour at its best. The contrasting texture of crisp dessert biscuits makes them the perfect accompaniment.

SERVES 4–6

250g/9oz/generous 2 cups strawberries
115g/4oz/scant 1/2 cup strawberry jam
250g/9oz/generous 1 cup ricotta cheese
200g/7oz/scant 1 cup Greek (strained plain) yogurt

5ml/1 tsp natural vanilla extract
40g/1 1/2 oz/3 tbsp caster (superfine) sugar
extra strawberries and mint or lemon balm, to decorate

1 Put the strawberries in a bowl and mash them with a fork until broken into small pieces but not completely puréed. Stir in the strawberry jam. Drain off any whey from the ricotta.

2 Tip the ricotta into a bowl and stir in the Greek yogurt, natural vanilla extract and sugar. Using a dessertspoon, gently fold the mashed strawberries into the ricotta mixture until rippled.

3 Spoon into individual freezerproof dishes and freeze for at least 2 hours until almost solid. Alternatively freeze until completely solid, then transfer the ice cream to the fridge for about 45 minutes to soften before serving. Serve in small bowls with extra strawberries and decorated with mint or lemon balm.

Nutritional information per portion: Energy 181kcal/764kJ; Protein 5.8g; Carbohydrate 29.6g, of which sugars 29.6g; Fat 5.3g, of which saturates 3.2g; Cholesterol 15mg; Calcium 91mg; Fibre 0.9g; Sodium 43mg.

Iced melon with Pimm's

The novel presentation and refreshing flavour of freezing sorbet in hollowed-out fruit – which is then cut into icy wedges – is simply irresistible on a hot summer's afternoon.

SERVES 6

50g/2oz/¼ cup caster (superfine) sugar
30ml/2 tbsp clear honey
15ml/1 tbsp lemon juice
60ml/4 tbsp water
1 medium cantaloupe or Charentais
   melon, about 1 kg/2¼lb
crushed ice, cucumber slices and borage
   leaves, to decorate
Pimm's No. 1, to serve

1 Gently heat the sugar, honey, lemon juice and water in a small, heavy pan until the sugar dissolves. Bring to the boil and boil for 1 minute, without stirring, to make a syrup. Leave to cool.

2 Cut the melon in half, discarding the seeds. Scoop the flesh into a food processor or blender, taking care to keep the shells intact.

3 Blend the flesh until smooth. Then transfer to a bowl, stir in the cooled syrup and chill in the refrigerator until very cold. Invert the melon shells and leave them to drain on kitchen paper. Then transfer to the freezer while making the sorbet.

4 Pour the mixture into a container and freeze for 3-4 hours, beating twice with a fork, a whisk or in a food processor, to break up the ice crystals.

5 Pack the sorbet into the melon shells and level the surface with a knife. Then use a dessertspoon to scoop out the centre of each filled melon shell to simulate the seed cavity. Freeze overnight until firm.

6 To serve, use a large knife to cut each half into three wedges. Serve on a bed of ice on a large platter or individual serving plates, and decorate with the cucumber slices and borage. Drizzle lightly with Pimm's to serve.

Nutritional information per portion: Energy 87kcal/ 372kJ; Protein 0.9g; Carbohydrate 21.9g, of which sugars 21.9g; Fat 0.2g, of which saturates 0g; Cholesterol 0mg; Calcium 26mg; Fibre 0.7g; Sodium 53mg.

Iced clementines

These pretty, sorbet-filled fruits store well in the freezer and are perfect for an impromptu summer party or a picnic, or simply a refreshing treat whenever you feel like it.

MAKES 12

16 large clementines
175g/6oz/scant 1 cup caster
     (superfine) sugar
105ml/7 tbsp water
juice of 2 lemons
a little fresh orange juice (if necessary)
fresh mint or lemon balm leaves,
     to decorate

5 Pour into a shallow container and freeze for 3-4 hours, beating twice. Then pack the sorbet into the clementine shells, position the lids and freeze overnight.

6 To soften the clementines, transfer them to the fridge about 30 minutes before serving on individual plates, decorated with fresh mint or lemon balm leaves.

Nutritional information per portion: Energy 77kcal/329kJ; Protein 0.6g; Carbohydrate 19.9g, of which sugars 19.9g; Fat 0.1g, of which saturates 0g; Cholesterol 0mg; Calcium 24mg; Fibre 0.6g; Sodium 3mg.

1 Slice the tops off 12 of the clementines to make lids. Set aside on a baking sheet. Scoop the flesh into a bowl, keeping the shells intact. Scrape out as much membrane as possible. Add the shells to the lids and put them in the freezer.

2 Gently heat and stir the sugar and water in a heavy pan until the sugar dissolves. Boil for 3 minutes without stirring. Cool. Stir in the lemon juice.

3 Finely grate the rind from the remaining clementines. Squeeze the fruits and add the juice and rind to the syrup.

4 Process the clementine flesh in a food processor/blender, then strain through a sieve (strainer) over a bowl. Add this to the syrup. You need about 900ml/1½ pints/3¾ cups of liquid. Top up with fresh orange juice if necessary.

Simple strawberry ice cream

Capture the essence of childhood summers with this easy-to-make ice cream. Whipping cream is a good choice for this recipe, as it doesn't overwhelm the taste of the fresh fruit.

SERVES 4–6

500g/1¼lb/4 cups strawberries, hulled
50g/2oz/½ cup icing
(confectioners') sugar
juice of ½ lemon
300ml/½ pint/1¼ cups whipping cream
extra strawberries, to decorate

1 Purée the strawberries in a food processor or blender until smooth then add the icing sugar and lemon juice and process again to mix. Press the purée through a sieve (strainer) into a bowl. Chill until very cold.

2 Whip the cream until it is just thickened but still falls from a spoon. Fold into the purée, then pour into a plastic tub or similar freezerproof container. Freeze for 6 hours until firm, beating twice with a fork, electric whisk or in a food processor to break up the ice crystals.

3 To serve, scoop into dishes and decorate with a few extra strawberries.

COOK'S TIP
If possible, taste the strawberries before buying them. Halve large strawberries for decoration.

Nutritional information per portion: Energy 244kcal/1012kJ; Protein 2.4g; Carbohydrate 12.2g, of which sugars 10.4g; Fat 20.4g, of which saturates 12.1g; Cholesterol 51mg; Calcium 73mg; Fibre 0.7g; Sodium 32mg.

Apricot and amaretti ice cream

Prolong apricots' short season by transforming them into this superb ice cream with crushed amaretti, whipped cream and, if you like, a few drops of amaretto liqueur.

SERVES 4–6

500g/1¼lb fresh apricots, halved and
   stoned (pitted)
juice of 1 orange
50g/2oz/¼ cup caster (superfine) sugar
300ml/½ pint/1¼ cups whipping cream
50g/2oz amaretti

1 Cover and simmer the apricots, orange juice and sugar in a pan for 5 minutes until the fruit is tender. Leave to cool.

2 Lift out one third of the fruit and set aside on a plate. Tip the remainder into a food processor or blender and process to a smooth purée.

3 Whip the cream until thick but soft enough to fall from a spoon. Slowly add the fruit purée, folding it into the mixture. Pour into a freezerproof container and freeze for 4 hours, beating once.

4 Beat a second time and then cumble in the amaretti.

5 Gently fold the reserved apricots into the ice cream. Freeze for 2–3 hours.

Nutritional information per portion: Energy 289kcal/1202kJ; Protein 2.3g; Carbohydrate 23.4g, of which sugars 19.8g; Fat 21.3g, of which saturates 13.1g; Cholesterol 53mg; Calcium 58mg; Fibre 1.6g; Sodium 43mg.

Blackberry ice cream

There could scarcely be fewer ingredients in this delicious and vibrantly coloured ice cream, which is sweet yet pleasantly refreshing.

SERVES 4–6

500g/1¼lb/5 cups blackberries, hulled, plus extra, to decorate
75g/3oz/6 tbsp caster (superfine) sugar
30ml/2 tbsp water
300ml/½ pint/1¼ cups whipping cream
crisp dessert biscuits, to serve

1 Cover and simmer the blackberries, sugar and water in a pan for 5 minutes.

2 Tip the fruit into a sieve (strainer) over a bowl and press through with a wooden spoon. Leave to cool, then chill.

3 Whip the cream until just thick but soft enough to fall from a spoon, then mix it with the fruit purée. Pour into a freezerproof container and freeze for 2 hours.

4 Mash the mixture with a fork to break up the ice crystals. Return to the freezer for 4 hours more, beating again after 2 hours.

5 Decorate with blackberries and serve in dishes with crisp dessert biscuits.

Nutritional information per portion: Energy 261kcal/1081kJ; Protein 1.8g; Carbohydrate 18.7g, of which sugars 18.7g; Fat 20.3g, of which saturates 12.6g; Cholesterol 53mg; Calcium 70mg; Fibre 2.6g; Sodium 15mg.

Gooseberry and clotted cream ice cream

The gooseberry can often be a rather neglected fruit but this indulgent ice cream puts it in a totally different class. Its delicious, slightly tart flavour goes particularly well with tiny, melt-in-the-mouth meringues.

SERVES 4–6

500g/1¼lb/4 cups gooseberries,
   topped and tailed
60ml/4 tbsp water
75g/3oz/6 tbsp caster (superfine) sugar
150ml/¼ pint/²⁄₃ cup whipping cream

a few drops of green food colouring
   (optional)
120ml/4fl oz/½ cup clotted cream
fresh mint sprigs, to decorate
meringues, to serve

1 Put the gooseberries in a pan and add the water and sugar. Then cover and simmer for 10 minutes or until soft. Pour into a food processor or blender and process to a smooth purée. Press through a sieve (strainer) placed over a bowl. Cool, then chill.

2 Chill the purée in a plastic tub or similar container. Whip the cream until it is thick but still falls from a spoon. Fold into the purée with the green food colouring, if you are using it.

3 Freeze for 2 hours, then beat with a fork or blender, or in a food processor to break up. Return to the freezer for 2 hours. Beat the ice cream again, then fold in the clotted cream. Then freeze for 2–3 hours.

4 To serve, scoop the ice cream into dishes or small plates, decorate with fresh mint sprigs and add a few small meringues to each serving.

Nutritional information per portion: Energy 278kcal/1152kJ; Protein 1.8g; Carbohydrate 16.7g, of which sugars 16.7g; Fat 23.1g, of which saturates 14.3g; Cholesterol 60mg; Calcium 52mg; Fibre 2g; Sodium 12mg.

Rhubarb and ginger ice cream

Here, the classic combination of gently poached rhubarb and chopped ginger is brought up to date by blending it with mascarpone to make this pretty blush-pink ice cream.

SERVES 4–6

5 pieces of preserved stem ginger
450g/1lb trimmed rhubarb, sliced
115g/4oz/¹⁄₂ cup caster
   (superfine) sugar
30ml/2 tbsp water
150g/5oz/²⁄₃ cup mascarpone
150ml/¹⁄₄ pint/²⁄₃ cup whipping cream
wafer cups, to serve (optional)

1 Using a sharp knife, roughly chop the stem ginger and set it aside. Put the rhubarb slices into a pan and add the sugar and water. Cover and simmer for 5 minutes until the rhubarb is just tender and still bright pink.

2 Tip the mixture into a food processor or blender, process until smooth, then leave to cool. Chill, if time permits.

3 Mix together the mascarpone, cream, ginger and rhubarb purée.

4 Pour the mixture into a plastic tub or other freezerproof container and freeze for 6 hours or until firm, beating once or twice with a fork or an electric whisk to break up the ice crystals.

5 Serve as scoops, either in bowls or wafer baskets.

Nutritional information per portion: Energy 221kcal/924kJ; Protein 3.6g; Carbohydrate 22.1g, of which sugars 22.1g; Fat 13.8g, of which saturates 8.6g; Cholesterol 37mg; Calcium 94mg; Fibre 1.1g; Sodium 10mg.

Mango and passion fruit gelato

Fresh and fruity, this tropical ice cream has a delicate perfume. Passion fruit tend to vary in size but if you can find some large ones, four should be plenty for this dish.

SERVES 4

4 large mangoes
grated rind and juice of 1 lime
50g/2oz/¹/₄ cup caster (superfine) sugar
300ml/¹/₂ pint/1¹/₄ cups whipping cream
4–6 passion fruit

1 Cut a thick slice from either side of the stone (pit) on each unpeeled mango. Using a sharp knife, make criss-cross cuts in the mango flesh.

2 Turn the slices inside out and scoop the pieces into a food processor. Cut the remaining flesh away from the stones (pits) and add it to the rest.

3 Process the flesh until smooth, then add the grated lime rind, lime juice and caster sugar. Process briefly.

4 Whip the cream until it is just thick but still falls from a spoon. Fold in the puréed mango and lime mixture, then freeze in a plastic tub or other freezerproof container for 4 hours until it is semi-frozen.

5 Cut the passion fruit in half and scoop the seeds and pulp into the ice cream mixture. Mix well and freeze for 2 hours until firm enough to scoop.

Nutritional information per portion: Energy 426kcal/1777kJ; Protein 3g; Carbohydrate 37.1g, of which sugars 36.7g; Fat 30.6g, of which saturates 19.1g; Cholesterol 79mg; Calcium 70mg; Fibre 4.4g; Sodium 25mg.

Nougat ice cream

Inspired by the delicious sweetmeats served in France as one of 13 traditional Christmas desserts, this is a superb ice cream, especially when served with iced liqueurs as iced petits fours.

SERVES 6–8

50g/2oz/¹⁄₂ cup hazelnuts
50g/2oz/¹⁄₂ cup pistachio nuts
50g/2oz/¹⁄₃ cup candied peel,
   in large pieces
6–8 sheets rice paper

3 egg whites
150g/5oz/1¹⁄₄ cups icing (confectioners')
   sugar, sifted
300ml/¹⁄₂ pint/1¹⁄₄ cups double
   (heavy) cream
10ml/2 tsp orange flower water

1 Spread the hazelnuts on a baking sheet and brown lightly under a hot grill (broiler). Mix them with the pistachio nuts and chop all the nuts roughly. Slice the candied peel thinly then cut the slices into bitesize slivers.

2 Line the base and sides of a 28 x 18 x 4cm/11 x 7 x 1¹⁄₂ in cake tin (pan) with clear film (plastic wrap), then with four of the pieces of rice paper, folding the paper into the corners and overlapping the sheets slightly.

3 Whisk the egg whites and icing sugar in a heatproof bowl placed over a pan of simmering water for 5 minutes or until the meringue is very thick.

4 Take off the heat and continue whisking until soft peaks form. In a separate bowl, whip the cream and orange flower water lightly, then fold in the meringue. Spoon half the meringue mixture into the lined cake tin, easing it into the corners.

5 Sprinkle the meringue with half the nuts and candied peel. Then cover with the remaining meringue mixture.

6 Sprinkle with the remaining nuts and fruit. Cover with two more sheets of rice paper and freeze for at least 6 hours or overnight until completely firm.

7 Carefully turn the ice cream out of the tin and peel off the clear film. If the base of the ice cream is soft, cover it with the remaining two sheets of rice paper, pressing it on to the ice cream so that it sticks. Cut into small squares or triangles, arrange on individual plates and serve.

Nutritional information per portion: Energy 380kcal/1579kJ; Protein 4.2g; Carbohydrate 29.8g, of which sugars 24.5g; Fat 27.7g, of which saturates 13.3g; Cholesterol 51mg; Calcium 54mg; Fibre 1.2g; Sodium 84mg.

Banana and toffee ice cream

The addition of sweetened condensed milk helps to bring out the natural flavour of the bananas and, surprisingly, the ice cream is not excessively sweet.

SERVES 4–6

3 ripe bananas
juice of 1 lemon
**370g/12¹/₂oz can sweetened
   condensed milk**
150ml/¹/₄ pint/²/₃ cup whipping cream
150g/5oz toffees
chopped toffees, to decorate

1 Process the bananas to a purée in a food processor or blender, then add the lemon juice and process briefly to mix. Scrape the purée into a plastic tub or similar freezerproof container.

2 Pour in the condensed milk, stirring with a metal spoon, then add the cream. Mix well, cover and freeze for 4 hours or until mushy.

3 Unwrap the toffees and chop them finely, using a sharp knife. If this proves difficult, put them in a double plastic bag and hit them with a rolling pin.

4 Beat the semi-frozen ice cream with a fork or electric mixer to break up the ice crystals, then stir in the toffees. Return the ice cream to the freezer for 3–5 hours or until firm. Scoop on to a plate or into a bowl and decorate with chopped toffees. Serve at once.

Nutritional information per portion: Energy 455kcal/1909kJ; Protein 6.9g; Carbohydrate 63.2g, of which sugars 56.6g; Fat 21.1g, of which saturates 12.6g; Cholesterol 53mg; Calcium 215mg; Fibre 0.6g; Sodium 178mg.

Rum and raisin ice cream

For many, this ice cream always seemed so much more sophisticated than mere vanilla. The longer you can leave the raisins to soak in the rum, the stronger the flavour will be.

SERVES 4–6

150g/5oz/scant 1 cup large raisins
60ml/4 tbsp dark rum
4 egg yolks
75g/3oz/6 tbsp light muscovado (brown) sugar
5ml/1 tsp cornflour (cornstarch)
300ml/½ pint/1¼ cups semi-skimmed (low-fat) milk
300ml/½ pint/1¼ cups whipping cream
dessert biscuits or ice cream cones, to serve

1 Leave the raisins soaking in the rum in a bowl for 3–4 hours or overnight.

2 Whisk the egg yolks, muscovado sugar and cornflour in a bowl until thick and foamy. In a heavy pan, bring the milk to just below boiling point.

3 Gradually whisk the milk into the eggs, then pour the mixture back into the pan. Cook gently, stirring constantly until thick and smooth. Take off the heat and leave to cool.

4 Whip the cream until it is thick but still falls from a spoon. Fold it into the custard and pour the mixture into a freezerproof container. Freeze for 4 hours, beating once with a fork or in a food processor. Then beat again.

5 Fold the soaked raisins into the ice cream, cover and freeze for 2–3 hours or until firm enough to scoop. Serve in bowls or tall glasses with dessert biscuits, or serve simply in ice cream cones.

Nutritional information per portion: Energy 397kcal/1654kJ; Protein 5.2g; Carbohydrate 34.9g, of which sugars 34.1g; Fat 24.8g, of which saturates 14.2g; Cholesterol 190mg; Calcium 123mg; Fibre 0.5g; Sodium 56mg.

Apricot parfait

In this delicious treat, pots of creamy, delicately flavoured French-style ice cream conceal a hidden layer of poached apricots.

SERVES 6

200g/7oz/scant 1 cup dried apricots
300ml/½ pint/1¼ cups apple juice
75g/3oz/6 tbsp demerara (raw) sugar
4 egg yolks

115g/4oz/generous ½ cup caster
  (superfine) sugar
120ml/4fl oz/½ cup water
150ml/¼ pint/⅔ cup whipping cream
grated rind and juice of ½ lemon

1 Put the apricots in a pan. Pour over the apple juice and soak for 3–4 hours. Line a baking sheet with foil. Using an inverted ramekin, draw six circles on the foil. Brush with a little oil.

2 Preheat the grill to its lowest setting. Sprinkle the demerara sugar into the circles. Place under the grill, on its lowest shelf setting and leave for 3–4 minutes until the sugar has melted and caramelized. Leave to cool and harden.

3 Simmer the apricots for 10 minutes until soft. Leave to cool, then lift out nine with a slotted spoon. Chop these apricots roughly and divide them among six freezerproof ramekins. Purée the remaining apricots and juice until smooth.

4 Whisk the egg yolks in a large, heatproof bowl until frothy. Gently heat the caster sugar and water in a pan until the sugar has dissolved, then boil for 4–5 minutes, until the syrup registers 119°C/238°F on a sugar thermometer. Alternatively, test by dropping a little of the syrup into a cup of cold water. Pour the water away. The syrup should mould into a soft ball.

5 Quickly whisk the hot syrup into the egg yolks. Put the bowl over a pan of simmering water and whisk the mixture until it is thick. Lift the bowl off the pan and continue whisking the mixture until it is cool and the whisk leaves a trail when lifted.

6 Whip the cream lightly, fold it into the yolk mixture, then gently fold in the apricot purée, with the lemon rind and juice.

7 Pour the parfait mixture into the six ramekins and freeze for 4 hours until firm. When ready to serve, roughly break the caramelized sugar into chunky pieces and use to decorate the ices.

Nutritional information per portion: Energy 257kcal/1077kJ; Protein 3.9g; Carbohydrate 30.9g, of which sugars 30.9g; Fat 14g, of which saturates 7.4g; Cholesterol 161mg; Calcium 65mg; Fibre 2.1g; Sodium 19mg.

Rocky road ice cream

This classic American ice cream is a mouthwatering combination of roughly crushed mixed-nut praline, rich vanilla custard and whipping cream.

SERVES 4–6

4 egg yolks
5ml/1 tsp cornflour (cornstarch)
225g/8oz/generous 1 cup sugar
300ml/½ pint/1¼ cups semi-skimmed (low-fat) milk
10ml/2 tsp natural vanilla extract

oil, for greasing
50g/2oz/½ cup macadamia nuts
50g/2oz/½ cup hazelnuts
50g/2oz/½ cup flaked (sliced) almonds
60ml/4 tbsp water
300ml/½ pint/1¼ cups whipping cream

1 In a bowl, stir the yolks, cornflour and 75g/3oz/6 tbsp of sugar. Whisk until thick and foamy. Bring the milk to the boil in a heavy pan, then whisk into the mixture in the bowl.

2 Return the mixture to the pan. Cook gently, stirring constantly until thick and smooth. Pour it back into the bowl and stir in the vanilla extract. Leave to cool, then chill.

3 Grease a large baking sheet with oil. Put the remaining sugar in a large, heavy frying pan, sprinkle the nuts on top and pour over the water. Heat gently, without stirring, until the sugar has dissolved completely, then boil the syrup for 3–5 minutes until just turning golden.

4 Quickly pour the nut mixture on to the oiled baking sheet and leave to cool and harden. Whip the cream until it is thick but still falls from a spoon. Fold it into the custard and freeze in a freezerproof container for 4 hours, beating once with a fork or electric whisk, and then beat again.

5 Break off about a third of the praline and keep for decoration. In a strong plastic bag, break the rest of it into bitesize pieces with a rolling pin.

6 Fold the crushed praline into the ice cream and freeze it for 2–3 hours until firm. Scoop into glasses and decorate with the reserved praline, broken into large pieces.

Nutritional information per portion: Energy 545kcal/2271kJ; Protein 4.7g; Carbohydrate 48.3g, of which sugars 40.6g; Fat 38.4g, of which saturates 22g; Cholesterol 77mg; Calcium 85mg; Fibre 1g; Sodium 57mg.

Maple and pecan nut ice cream

This American ice cream is even more delicious when served with extra maple syrup and topped with whole pecan nuts. For best results, use "pure maple syrup" not "maple-flavoured" syrup.

SERVES 4–6

115g/4oz/1 cup pecan nuts
4 egg yolks
50g/2oz/¼ cup caster (superfine) sugar
5ml/1 tsp cornflour (cornstarch)
300ml/½ pint/1¼ cups semi-skimmed (low-fat) milk
60ml/4 tbsp maple syrup
300ml/½ pint/1¼ cups whipping cream
extra maple syrup and pecan nuts, to serve

1 Cut the pecan nuts in half lengthways, spread them out on a baking sheet and grill (broil) them under a moderate heat for 2–3 minutes until lightly browned. Remove from the heat and cool.

2 Place the egg yolks, sugar and cornflour into a bowl and whisk until thick and foamy. Pour the milk into a heavy pan, bring to the boil, then gradually whisk it into the yolk mixture.

3 Return the mixture to the pan and cook over a gentle heat, stirring constantly until the custard thickens and is smooth.

4 Pour the custard back into the bowl, and stir in the maple syrup. Leave to cool, then chill.

5 Whip the cream until it is thick but still falls from a spoon. Fold it into the custard and freeze in a freezerproof container for 4 hours, beating once with a fork or electric whisk to break up the ice crystals. Then, beat it again.

6 Fold in the nuts. Freeze for 2–3 hours until firm enough to scoop into dishes. Pour extra maple syrup over each portion and top with extra pecan nuts.

Nutritional information per portion: Energy 429kcal/1777kJ; Protein 4.8g; Carbohydrate 19.8g, of which sugars 18.8g; Fat 37.3g, of which saturates 14.8g; Cholesterol 187mg; Calcium 63mg; Fibre 0.9g; Sodium 47mg.

Cashew and orange flower ice cream

Delicately perfumed with orange flower water and a little orange rind, this nutty, lightly sweetened ice cream evokes images of puddings that are popular in the Middle East.

SERVES 4–6

4 egg yolks
75g/3oz/6 tbsp caster (superfine) sugar
5ml/1 tsp cornflour (cornstarch)
300ml/½ pint/1¼ cups semi-skimmed (low-fat) milk
300ml/½ pint/1¼ cups whipping cream
150g/5oz/1¼ cups cashew nuts, finely chopped
15ml/1 tbsp orange flower water
grated rind of ½ orange, plus curls of thinly pared orange rind, to decorate

1 Whisk the egg yolks, caster sugar and cornflour in a bowl until thick and foamy. Pour the semi-skimmed milk into a heavy pan, gently bring it to the boil, then gradually whisk it into the egg yolk mixture.

2 Return to the pan and cook gently, stirring constantly until smooth. Pour back into the bowl. Cool, then chill.

3 Heat the cream in a pan. When it boils, stir in the chopped cashew nuts. Leave to cool.

4 Stir the orange flower water and grated orange rind into the chilled custard. Process the nut cream in a food processor or blender to form a fine paste. Stir into the custard mixture.

5 Then pour the mixture into a tub and freeze for 6 hours, beating twice to break up the ice crystals.

6 To serve, scoop the ice cream into dishes and decorate each portion with an orange rind curl.

Nutritional information per portion: Energy 464kcal/1928kJ; Protein 9.9g; Carbohydrate 23g, of which sugars 18.2g; Fat 37.6g, of which saturates 16.8g; Cholesterol 197mg; Calcium 121mg; Fibre 0.8g; Sodium 115mg.

Pistachio ice cream

This European favourite owes its enduring popularity to its delicate pale green colour and distinctive yet subtle flavour. Buy the pistachio nuts as you need them, as they quickly go stale if left in the cupboard.

SERVES 4–6

4 egg yolks
75g/3oz/6 tbsp caster (superfine) sugar
5ml/1 tsp cornflour (cornstarch)
300ml/$\frac{1}{2}$ pint/1$\frac{1}{4}$ cups semi-skimmed (low-fat) milk

115g/4oz/1 cup pistachios, plus a few extra, to decorate
300ml/$\frac{1}{2}$ pint/1$\frac{1}{4}$ cups whipping cream
a little green food colouring
chocolate dipped waffle cones, to serve (optional)

1 Whisk the egg yolks, sugar and cornflour in a bowl until the mixture is thick and foamy.

2 In a heavy pan, gently bring the milk to the boil, then gradually whisk it into the egg yolk mixture.

3 Return the mixture to the pan and cook it over a gentle heat, stirring constantly until the custard thickens and is smooth. Pour it back into the bowl, set aside to cool, then chill in the refrigerator until required.

4 Shell the pistachios and put them in a food processor or blender. Add 30ml/2 tbsp of the cream and grind the mixture to a coarse paste.

5 Pour the rest of the cream into a small pan. Bring it to the boil, stir in the coarsely ground pistachios, then leave to cool.

6 Mix the chilled custard and pistachio cream together and tint the mixture delicately with a few drops of food colouring.

7 Pour the tinted custard and pistachio mixture into a plastic tub or similar freezerproof container. Freeze for 6 hours, beating once or twice with a fork or an electric whisk to break up the ice crystals. Scoop the ice cream into cones or dishes to serve and sprinkle each portion with a few extra pistachios.

Nutritional information per portion: Energy 422kcal/1749kJ; Protein 8.1g; Carbohydrate 19.1g, of which sugars 17.9g; Fat 35.3g, of which saturates 15.6g; Cholesterol 190mg; Calcium 133mg; Fibre 1.2g; Sodium 143mg.

Cream-free
& low-fat ices

Indulging in rich traditional ice creams is

not to everyone's taste. On the following

pages are some intensely-flavoured

desserts using low-fat and dairy-free

ingredients. With recipes that range

from a smooth, creamy coconut ice

to a refreshing orange and yogurt

ice, there is an iced dessert

to suit everyone.

Kulfi

This famous Indian ice cream is traditionally made by slowly boiling milk, reducing it by two-thirds. Although using condensed milk saves time, nothing beats this delicious ice cream made in the authentic manner.

SERVES 4

1.5 litres/2¹/₂ pints/6¹/₄ cups full-fat (whole) milk

3 cardamom pods

25g/1oz/2 tbsp caster (superfine) sugar

50g/2oz/¹/₂ cup pistachios, skinned plus a few to decorate

a few pink rose petals, to decorate

1 Pour the milk into a large, heavy pan. Bring to the boil, lower the heat and simmer gently for 1 hour, stirring occasionally.

2 Put the cardamom pods in a mortar and crush them with a pestle. Add the pods and the seeds to the milk and continue to simmer for 1–1¹/₂ hours or until the milk has reduced to about 475ml/16fl oz/2 cups.

3 Strain the milk into a jug, stir in the sugar and leave to cool.

4 Grind half the pistachios to a smooth powder in a blender, nut grinder or cleaned coffee grinder. Cut the remaining pistachios into thin slivers and set them aside for decoration. Stir the ground nuts into the milk mixture.

5 Pour the milk and pistachio mixture into four kulfi moulds. Freeze overnight until firm.

6 To unmould the kulfi, half fill a plastic container or bowl with very hot water, stand the moulds in the water and count to ten. Immediately lift out the moulds and invert them on a baking sheet.

7 Transfer the ice creams to a platter or individual plates. To decorate, scatter sliced pistachios over the ice creams and then the rose petals. Serve at once.

Nutritional information per portion: Energy 347kcal/1443kJ; Protein 14.7g; Carbohydrate 24.4g, of which sugars 24.1g; Fat 21.6g, of which saturates 10.3g; Cholesterol 53mg; Calcium 460mg; Fibre 0.8g; Sodium 228mg.

Date and tofu ice

Generously spiced with cinnamon, this creamy tofu treat not only tastes good but is packed with soya protein, contains no added sugar, is low in fat and free from all dairy products.

SERVES 4

250g/9oz/1¹/₂ cups stoned (pitted) dates
600ml/1 pint/2¹/₂ cups apple juice
5ml/1 tsp ground cinnamon
285g/10¹/₂oz pack chilled tofu, drained
    and cubed
150ml/¹/₄ pint/²/₃ cup unsweetened
    soya milk

1 Soak the dates in a pan, in 300ml/¹/₂ pint/1¹/₄ cups of apple juice for 2 hours. Simmer for 10 minutes, then leave to cool. With a slotted spoon, lift out a quarter of the dates, chop roughly and set aside.

2 Purée the remaining dates, plus any apple juice left in the pan, in a food processor. Add the cinnamon and more apple juice, and process to make a smooth paste.

3 Add the tofu cubes, a few at a time, processing each time. Add the remaining apple juice and soya milk.

4 Pour the mixture into a plastic container and freeze for 4 hours, beating once with a fork or mixer or in a food processor to break up the ice crystals.

5 After this time, beat again with a fork or mixer, or in a food processor, to ensure a smooth texture.

6 Stir in most of the chopped dates and freeze for 2–3 hours until firm.

7 Scoop into dessert glasses and decorate with the remaining chopped dates.

Nutritional information per portion: Energy 290kcal/1232kJ; Protein 9.1g; Carbohydrate 58.2g, of which sugars 57.9g; Fat 3.9g, of which saturates 0.5g; Cholesterol 0mg; Calcium 407mg; Fibre 2.5g; Sodium 24mg.

Dondurma kaymalki

As sahlab and mastic – two of the ingredients of this Middle Eastern ice cream – are difficult to obtain in the West, cornflour and condensed milk have been used in their place.

SERVES 4–6

45ml/3 tbsp cornflour (cornstarch)
600ml/1 pint/2¹/₂ cups full-fat (whole) milk
213g/7¹/₂ oz can sweetened condensed milk
15ml/1 tbsp clear honey
10ml/2 tsp orange flower water
a few sugared almonds, to serve

1 In a pan, mix the cornflour and a little milk to a smooth paste. Stir in the remaining milk and the condensed milk and bring to the boil, stirring until thickened and smooth. Pour into a bowl.

2 Stir in the honey and orange flower water. Cover with a plate to prevent a skin forming. Cool, then chill.

3 Pour the mixture into a plastic tub or similar freezerproof container and freeze for 6–8 hours, beating twice with a fork, electric mixer or in a food processor to break up the ice crystals.

4 To serve, scoop the ice cream into individual dishes and serve with a few sugared almonds.

Nutritional information per portion: Energy 218kcal/917kJ; Protein 6.4g; Carbohydrate 33g, of which sugars 26.1g; Fat 7.5g, of which saturates 4.8g; Cholesterol 27mg; Calcium 222mg; Fibre 0g; Sodium 97mg.

Honeyed goat's milk gelato

Goat's milk is more widely available than it used to be and is more easily tolerated by some people than cow's milk. It makes a surprisingly rich iced dessert.

SERVES 4

6 egg yolks

50g/2oz/¼ cup caster (superfine) sugar

10ml/2 tsp cornflour (cornstarch)

600ml/1 pint/2½ cups goat's milk

60ml/4 tbsp clear honey

pomegranate seeds, to decorate

1 Whisk the egg yolks, sugar and cornflour in a bowl until pale and thick. Pour the goat's milk into a heavy pan, bring it to the boil, and then gradually whisk it into the yolk mixture.

2 Return the custard mixture to the pan and cook over a gentle heat, stirring constantly until the custard thickens and is smooth. Pour it back into the clean bowl.

3 Stir the honey into the milk mixture. Leave to cool, then chill.

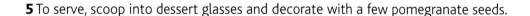

4 Pour the mixture into a plastic tub or similar freezerproof container and freeze for 6 hours until firm enough to scoop, beating twice with a fork, electric whisk or in a food processor to break up the ice crystals.

5 To serve, scoop into dessert glasses and decorate with a few pomegranate seeds.

VARIATION

This ice cream is also delicious with a little ginger; stir in 40g/1½oz/¼ cup finely chopped preserved stem ginger when the ice cream is partially frozen.

Nutritional information per portion: Energy 255kcal/1075kJ; Protein 7.7g; Carbohydrate 33.4g, of which sugars 31.1g; Fat 11.1g, of which saturates 5.1g; Cholesterol 218mg; Calcium 181mg; Fibre 0g; Sodium 76mg.

Raspberry fromage frais sherbet

This modern version of a sherbet is made from raspberry purée blended with sugar syrup and virtually fat-free fromage frais, then flecked with crushed raspberries.

SERVES 6

175g/6oz/³/₄ cup caster
   (superfine) sugar
150ml/¹/₄ pint/²/₃ cup water
500g/1¹/₄lb/3¹/₂ cups raspberries, plus
   extra, to serve
500ml/17fl oz/generous 2 cups virtually
   fat-free fromage frais (low-fat
   cream cheese)

1 Put the sugar and water in a small pan and bring to the boil, stirring until the sugar has dissolved. Pour into a jug and cool.

2 Process 350g/12oz/2¹/₂ cups of raspberries in a food processor or blender to a purée, then strain over a large bowl to remove the seeds, pressing with a wooden spoon. Stir in the sugar syrup and chill the mixture until it is very cold. Then add the fromage frais to the purée and whisk until smooth.

3 Pour the mixture into a freezerproof container and freeze for 4 hours, beating once with a fork, electric whisk or in a food processor to break up the ice crystals. Then, beat it again.

4 Crush the remaining raspberries between your fingers and add them to the partially frozen ice cream. Mix lightly then freeze for 2–3 hours until firm. Scoop the ice cream into dishes and serve with extra raspberries.

Nutritional information per portion: Energy 276kcal/1181kJ; Protein 11.6g; Carbohydrate 60g, of which sugars 60g; Fat 0.6g, of which saturates 0.3g; Cholesterol 1mg; Calcium 163mg; Fibre 3.1g; Sodium 48mg.

Orange and yogurt ice

Serve this refreshing low-fat yogurt ice simply, in cones, or scoop it into bought meringue nests and decorate with blueberries and mint for a more sophisticated treat.

SERVES 6

90ml/6 tbsp water
10ml/2 tsp powdered gelatine
115g/4oz/½ cup caster
    (superfine) sugar
250ml/8fl oz/1 cup "freshly squeezed"
    orange juice from a carton or bottle
500ml/17fl oz/generous 2 cups
    natural (plain) yogurt
cones or meringue nests, blueberries and
    fresh mint sprigs, to serve

1 Put 30ml/2 tbsp of the water in a bowl and sprinkle the powdered gelatine over the top. Set aside until spongy. Meanwhile, put the sugar in a small pan, add the remaining water and heat through gently until the sugar has completely dissolved.

2 Take off the heat, add the gelatine and stir until dissolved. Cool, stir in the orange juice and chill for 15–30 minutes.

3 Spoon the yogurt into a bowl, gradually add the chilled orange juice and syrup mixture and mix well. Pour into a plastic tub. Freeze for 6 hours or until firm, beating twice with a fork or in a food processor to break up the ice crystals.

4 Scoop the yogurt into ice cones or meringue nests and decorate with blueberries and mint.

Nutritional information per portion: Energy 137kcal/583kJ; Protein 4.6g; Carbohydrate 30g, of which sugars 30g; Fat 0.9g, of which saturates 0.4g; Cholesterol 1mg; Calcium 173mg; Fibre 0.1g; Sodium 75mg.

Coconut ice

Despite its creamy taste, this ice contains neither cream nor egg and is, in fact, very refreshing. Decorate with thin slices of toasted coconut.

SERVES 4–6

150ml/¼ pint/⅔ cup water
115g/4oz/½ cup caster (superfine) sugar
2 limes

400ml/14fl oz can coconut milk
toasted coconut shavings, to decorate
    (see Cook's Tip)

1 Put the water in a small pan. Tip in the caster sugar and bring to the boil, stirring constantly until the sugar has all dissolved. Remove the pan from the heat and leave the syrup to cool, then chill well.

2 Grate the limes finely, taking care to avoid the bitter pith. Squeeze them and pour the juice and rind into the pan of syrup. Add the coconut milk.

3 Pour the mixture into a plastic tub or similar freezerproof container and freeze for 5–6 hours until firm, beating twice with a fork, electric whisk or in a food processor to break up the crystals. Scoop into dishes and decorate with toasted coconut shavings.

COOK'S TIP
Use the flesh from a coconut to make a pretty decoration. Having rinsed the flesh with cold water, cut off thin slices using a swivel-bladed vegetable peeler. Toast the slices under a moderate grill (broiler) until the coconut has curled and the edges have turned golden. Cool slightly, then sprinkle the shavings over the coconut ice.

Nutritional information per portion: Energy 90kcal/386kJ; Protein 0.3g; Carbohydrate 23.3g, of which sugars 23.3g; Fat 0.2g, of which saturates 0.1g; Cholesterol 0mg; Calcium 30mg; Fibre 0g; Sodium 75mg.

Bombes, terrines, tortes & gâteaux

Iced tortes and gâteaux make an impressive finale to any dinner party, and are easy to make. Layered, marbled or speckled with fruit and nuts, bombes and terrines make stunning iced desserts that reveal a feast of colour and texture when cut open.

Raspberry cranachan bombe

The flavours in this recipe stem from a traditional Scottish dessert comprising a whisky and honey flavoured cream with toasted oatmeal and raspberries.

SERVES 8

750ml/1¼ pints/3 cups Raspberry Sorbet
550ml/18fl oz/2½ cups double (heavy) cream
60ml/4 tbsp clear honey
75ml/5 tbsp whisky
50g/2oz/½ cup medium oatmeal, toasted

1 Soften the sorbet slightly by letting it stand at room temperature for about 20 minutes. Meanwhile, chill a 1.5 litre/2½ pint/6¼ cup bombe mould or bowl.

2 Using a large spoon, evenly pack the sorbet on to the base and up the sides of the mould. If this proves difficult and the sorbet starts to slide around, freeze it for about 10 minutes before continuing. Return the bombe mould to the freezer.

3 Whip the cream with the honey and whisky until it forms soft peaks, then fold in the oatmeal. Spoon into the sorbet-lined mould and level the surface. Cover with clear film (plastic wrap) and freeze overnight.

4 To serve, loosen the edges of the mould with a knife. Dip the mould very briefly in hot water, then invert on to a serving plate. Serve in wedges.

VARIATION
Cointreau or another orange-flavoured liqueur could be used instead of whisky. If preferred, 75g/3oz/¾ cup finely chopped and toasted hazelnuts could be substituted for the oatmeal.

Nutritional information per portion: Energy 518kcal/2158kJ; Protein 3g; Carbohydrate 39.2g, of which sugars 34.6g; Fat 37.7g, of which saturates 23g; Cholesterol 94mg; Calcium 68mg; Fibre 2.2g; Sodium 22mg.

Cassata

An irresistible Italian ice cream, cassata usually comprises three layers frozen in a bombe mould. This version combines the complementary flavours of pistachio, vanilla and tutti frutti.

SERVES 8

6 egg yolks

225g/8oz/generous 1 cup caster
  (superfine) sugar

15ml/1 tbsp cornflour (cornstarch)

600ml/1 pint/2¹/₂ cups milk

600ml/1 pint/2¹/₂ cups double
  (heavy) cream

75g/3oz/³/₄ cup pistachio nuts

2.5ml/¹/₂ tsp almond extract

dash each of green and red food colouring

40g/1¹/₂oz/¹/₄ cup candied peel,
  finely chopped

50g/2oz/¹/₄ cup glacé (candied) cherries,
  washed, dried and finely chopped

5ml/1 tsp vanilla extract

1 Whisk the egg yolks, sugar, cornflour and a little of the milk in a bowl until creamy. Bring the remaining milk and the cream to the boil in a heavy pan.

2 Pour into the egg yolk mixture in a steady stream, whisking well. Pour back into the pan. Cook gently, stirring until thickened, but do not boil. Remove from the heat and divide into three equal quantities. Cover and leave to cool.

3 Cover the pistachio nuts with boiling water in a bowl and leave for 1 minute. Drain and rub between several thicknesses of kitchen paper, to loosen the skins.

4 Roughly chop and add to one bowl with the almond extract and a drop of green food colouring.

5 Stir the candied peel, glacé cherries and a drop of red food colouring into the second bowl. Stir the vanilla extract into the third. Line a dampened 900g/2lb terrine or loaf tin (pan) with baking parchment.

6 Pour the mixtures into 3 separate tubs and freeze until thickened, beating twice. Put the frozen pistachio ice cream into the prepared tin, then the vanilla and the tutti frutti. Freeze overnight.

7 To serve, dip the terrine or tin in very hot water for 2–3 seconds, then place a long serving plate upside down on top of it. Holding together, turn them over. Lift off the container. Peel away the lining paper. Serve the cassata in slices.

Nutritional information per portion: Energy 380kcal/
1598kJ; Protein 9.3g; Carbohydrate 50.7g, of which
sugars 43.8g; Fat 13.3g, of which saturates 7.3g;
Cholesterol 97mg; Calcium 72mg; Fibre 1.9g;
Sodium 115mg.

Iced coconut mousse

Unlike most iced desserts, this is not custard-based. Instead, creamed coconut is folded into a light Italian-style meringue, producing a delicious mousse-like texture.

SERVES 6

4 medium egg whites
150g/5oz/³/₄ cup caster (superfine) sugar
175g/6oz/1¹/₂ cups creamed
   coconut, grated
300ml/¹/₂ pint/1¹/₄ cups double
   (heavy) cream
15ml/1 tbsp lemon juice
toasted coconut shavings, to decorate

FOR THE SAUCE
6 passion fruit
2.5ml/¹/₂ tsp cornflour (cornstarch)
150ml/¹/₄ pint/²/₃ cup fresh orange juice
15ml/1 tbsp caster (superfine) sugar
45ml/3 tbsp Kirsch

1 Dampen 6 150ml/¹/₄ pint/²/₃ cup metal moulds, and line with clear film (plastic wrap). Simmer the egg whites and sugar in a large, heatproof bowl over water in a pan. Beat with an electric whisk until the meringue mixture is very thick.

2 Remove from the heat and continue beating for about 2 minutes until the whisk leaves a thick trail when lifted.

3 Fold in the grated coconut. In a separate bowl, whip the cream until it forms soft peaks. Using a large metal spoon, fold the cream and lemon juice into the meringue. Spoon into the prepared moulds.

4 To level, draw a knife across the top of each mould. Cover with clear film and freeze for 4 hours or overnight.

5 For the sauce, cut the passion fruits in half and scoop the seeds and pulp into a small pan. Blend the cornflour with a little orange juice and stir into the passion fruit mixture, with the remaining orange juice and sugar. Heat gently, stirring until the mixture thickens slightly. Leave to cool, then stir in the Kirsch.

6 Dip each mould into very hot water for 1 second. Invert on dessert plates, lift off and peel away the film. Spoon over a little sauce, decorate with coconut shavings and serve.

Nutritional information per portion: Energy 593kcal/ 2464kJ; Protein 5.1g; Carbohydrate 37.2g, of which sugars 37.2g; Fat 47g, of which saturates 34g; Cholesterol 69mg; Calcium 51mg; Fibre 0.5g; Sodium 68mg.

Layered chocolate and chestnut bombes

These delicious bombes look very effective served on plates drizzled with melted plain chocolate.
Or, simply dust the plates with cocoa powder or scatter the bombes with grated chocolate.

SERVES 6

3 egg yolks
75g/3oz/6 tbsp caster (superfine) sugar
10ml/2 tsp cornflour (cornstarch)
300ml/½ pint/1¼ cups milk
115g/4oz plain (semisweet) chocolate,
   broken into pieces, plus 50g/2oz,
   to decorate

150g/5oz/½ cup sweetened
   chestnut purée
30ml/2 tbsp brandy or Cointreau
130g/4½oz/generous ½ cup mascarpone
5ml/1 tsp vanilla extract
450ml/¾ pint/scant 2 cups double
   (heavy) cream

1 In a bowl, whisk the egg yolks, the sugar, cornflour and a little milk. Bring the remaining milk to the boil in a heavy pan. Pour the milk over the egg mixture, whisking well. Return to the pan and cook gently, stirring until thickened but do not boil. Divide the custard equally among three bowls.

2 Add 115g/4oz of the chocolate to one bowl and leave to melt, stirring until smooth. If it fails to melt completely, microwave very briefly.

3 If the chestnut purée is firm, beat until soft and stir into the second bowl, with the brandy or Cointreau. Add the mascarpone and vanilla extract to the third bowl. Cover each closely with a circle of baking parchment and leave to cool.

4 Whip the cream into soft peaks and fold one-third into each of the custard mixtures. Share the chestnut mixture between 6 150ml/¼ pint/⅔ cup plain or fluted moulds and level the surface.

5 Spoon the chocolate mixture over the chestnut mixture in the moulds and level the surface. Spoon the vanilla mixture over the chocolate. Cover and freeze for 6 hours or overnight.

6 To serve, melt the chocolate for decoration in a heatproof bowl over a pan of gently simmering water. Transfer to a paper piping bag and snip off the tip. Or, use a piping bag fitted with a writing nozzle. Scribble lines of melted chocolate over the serving plates to decorate. Loosen the edge of each mould with a knife, dip very briefly in hot water, then invert on to a flat surface. Using a metal spatula, transfer the bombes to the serving plates. Leave for 10 minutes at room temperature before serving.

Nutritional information per portion: Energy 671kcal/2786kJ; Protein 7.9g; Carbohydrate 40.2g, of which sugars 31.1g; Fat 53.1g, of which saturates 31.7g; Cholesterol 217mg; Calcium 133mg; Fibre 1.5g; Sodium 48mg.

Spicy pumpkin and orange bombe

Ordinarily, pumpkin has a subtle flavour. However, you can truly transform it with the simple addition of citrus fruits and spices. Here, the delicious mixture is encased in syrupy sponge and served with an orange and whole spice syrup.

SERVES 8

FOR THE SPONGE

115g/4oz/¹/₂ cup unsalted (sweet)
     butter, softened
115g/4oz/¹/₂ cup caster (superfine) sugar
115g/4oz/1 cup self-raising (self-rising) flour
2.5ml/¹/₂ tsp baking powder
2 eggs

FOR THE ICE CREAM

1 orange
300g/11oz/scant 1¹/₂ cups soft light
     brown sugar

300ml/¹/₂ pint /1¹/₄ cups water
2 cinnamon sticks, halved
10ml/2 tsp whole cloves
30ml/2 tbsp orange flower water
400g/14oz can unsweetened pumpkin purée
300ml/¹/₂ pint/1¹/₄ cups extra thick double
     (heavy) cream
2 pieces preserved stem ginger, grated
icing (confectioners') sugar, for dusting

1 Preheat the oven to 180°C/350°F/Gas 4. Grease and line a 450g/1lb loaf tin (pan) with baking parchment. Beat the softened butter, caster sugar, flour, baking powder and eggs in a bowl until creamy.

2 Scrape the mixture into the prepared tin, level the surface and bake for 30–35 minutes until firm in the centre. Leave to cool.

3 Make the ice cream. Pare thin strips of rind from the orange; scrape off any white pith, then cut the strips into very fine shreds. Squeeze the orange and set the juice aside. Heat the sugar and water in a small, heavy pan until the sugar dissolves. Bring to the boil and boil rapidly without stirring for 3 minutes.

4 Stir in the orange shreds, juice, cinnamon and cloves and heat gently for 5 minutes. Strain the syrup, reserving the orange shreds and spices. Measure 300ml/¹/₂ pint/1¹/₄ cups of the syrup and reserve. Return the spices to the remaining syrup and stir in the orange flower water. Leave to cool in a jug.

5 Beat the pumpkin purée with 175ml/6fl oz/³/₄ cup of the measured strained syrup until evenly combined. Stir in the cream and ginger. Cut the cake into 1cm/¹/₂in slices. Dampen a 1.5 litre/2¹/₂ pint/6¹/₄ cup bowl and line it with clear film (plastic wrap). Pour the remaining strained syrup into a shallow dish.

6 Dip the cake slices briefly in the syrup and use to line the prepared bowl, placing the syrupy coated sides against the bowl. Trim the pieces to fit where necessary, so that the lining is even and any gaps are filled. Chill.

7 Pour the pumpkin mixture into a shallow container and freeze until firm. Scrape the ice cream into the sponge-lined bowl, level the surface and freeze until firm, preferably overnight.

8 To serve, invert the ice cream on to a serving plate. Lift off the bowl and peel away the clear film. Dust with the icing sugar and serve in wedges with the spiced syrup spooned over.

Nutritional information per portion: Energy 571kcal/2387kJ; Protein 4.2g; Carbohydrate 67g, of which sugars 56.1g; Fat 33.6g, of which saturates 20.5g; Cholesterol 130mg; Calcium 122mg; Fibre 1g; Sodium 168mg.

Rippled nectarine and muscovado terrine

This sumptuous combination of nectarine ice cream, cream cheese and brown sugar is set in the corner of a tilted square cake tin to create an interesting triangular shape.

SERVES 6–8

50g/2oz/¼ cup light muscovado (brown) sugar

7.5ml/1½ tsp hot water

200g/7oz/scant 1 cup cream cheese

115g/4oz/1 cup icing (confectioners') sugar

90ml/6 tbsp milk

3 ripe nectarines

10ml/2 tsp lemon juice

100ml/3½ fl oz/scant ½ cup extra thick double (heavy) cream

1 Line one half of a 20cm/8in square cake tin with clear film (plastic wrap). Dissolve the sugar in the water, stirring to form a syrup. Beat the cream cheese in a bowl with a quarter of the icing sugar until soft and smooth; then beat in the milk.

2 Halve and stone (pit) the nectarines and purée in a food processor with the lemon juice and remaining icing sugar.

3 Whip the cream, then fold in the purée. Prop the tin at a 45° angle. Spoon in a third of the nectarine purée. Place spoonfuls of the cream cheese mixture over the purée.

4 Drizzle with half the muscovado syrup. Spoon half the remaining nectarine mixture into the tin, then spoon over the remaining cream cheese, syrup and remaining nectarine mixture.

5 Using a dessertspoon handle, fold the mixtures together in about six strokes to lightly ripple the ingredients. Freeze overnight, keeping the tin propped at a 45° angle in the freezer; then lay flat.

6 Transfer to the fridge 30 minutes before serving so that it softens. Turn out on a serving plate and peel away the film. Serve in slices.

Nutritional information per portion: Energy 495kcal/2060kJ; Protein 2.6g; Carbohydrate 38.9g, of which sugars 38.7g; Fat 33.9g, of which saturates 20.9g; Cholesterol 70mg; Calcium 47mg; Fibre 1.7g; Sodium 16mg.

Caramel and pecan terrine

The combination of caramel and nuts in this dessert is really delicious. Take care that the syrup does not become too dark or the ice cream will taste bitter.

SERVES 6

115g/4oz/generous ¹/₂ cup sugar
75ml/5 tbsp water
450ml/³/₄ pint/scant 2 cups double
   (heavy) cream
30ml/2 tbsp icing (confectioners') sugar
75g/3oz/³/₄ cup pecan nuts, toasted

1 Heat the sugar and water in a small, heavy pan until the sugar dissolves. Boil rapidly until it turns pale golden. Leave to stand until it develops a rich brown colour.

2 Pour 90ml/6 tbsp of the cream over the caramel. Heat to make a smooth sauce. Leave to cool.

3 Dampen a 450g/1lb loaf tin (pan); line with clear film (plastic wrap). Whip 150ml/¹/₄ pint/²/₃ cup of cream with icing sugar into soft peaks. Whip the remaining cream separately. Stir in the caramel sauce and nuts.

4 Spoon a third of the caramel cream into the prepared loaf tin and spread with half the sugared whipped cream.

5 Spread half of the remaining caramel cream over the top, then top with the last of the sugared cream. Add the remaining caramel cream and level the surface. Freeze for 6 hours.

6 To serve, dip the tin in very hot water for 2 seconds, invert on to a serving plate and peel away the film. Serve sliced.

Nutritional information per portion: Energy 553kcal/2292kJ; Protein 2.5g; Carbohydrate 27.3g, of which sugars 27.1g; Fat 49g, of which saturates 25.8g; Cholesterol 103mg; Calcium 57mg; Fibre 0.6g; Sodium 18mg.

Mocha, prune and Armagnac terrine

This is a really simple iced dessert that is ideal for entertaining. Remember to allow time for the prunes to soak in the Armagnac, which is smoother and fruitier than ordinary brandy.

SERVES 6

115g/4oz/¹/₂ cup ready-to-eat pitted prunes, chopped
90ml/6 tbsp Armagnac
90g/3¹/₂oz/¹/₂ cup caster (superfine) sugar
150ml/¹/₄ pint/²/₃ cup water
45ml/3 tbsp coffee beans
150g/5oz plain (semisweet) chocolate, broken into pieces
300ml/¹/₂ pint/1¹/₄ cups double (heavy) cream
unsweetened cocoa powder, for dusting

1 Soak the prunes with 75ml/5 tbsp of the Armagnac in a small bowl, for 3 hours at room temperature, or overnight in the fridge. Line the bases of 6 100ml/3¹/₂fl oz/scant ¹/₂ cup ramekins with circles of baking parchment.

2 Gently heat the sugar and measured water in a pan until the sugar dissolves. Add the soaked prunes and any Armagnac left in the bowl; simmer for 5 minutes. Then, using a slotted spoon, lift the prunes out of the pan and set aside. Add the coffee beans to the syrup and simmer gently for 5 minutes.

3 Lift out the coffee beans and put about a third of them in a bowl. Spoon over 120ml/4fl oz/¹/₂ cup of the syrup and stir in the remaining Armagnac. Set aside until ready to serve.

4 Melt the chocolate in a pan with the remaining syrup. Whip the cream until it holds its shape. Fold the chocolate mixture and prunes into the cream. Spoon the mixture into the lined ramekins, cover and freeze for 3 hours. To serve, loosen the ramekin edges with a knife, dip in hot water for 2 seconds and invert on to serving plates. Decorate with coffee bean syrup and cocoa powder.

Nutritional information per portion: Energy 495kcal/2060kJ; Protein 2.6g; Carbohydrate 38.9g, of which sugars 38.7g; Fat 33.9g, of which saturates 20.9g; Cholesterol 70mg; Calcium 47mg; Fibre 1.7g; Sodium 16mg.

Marzipan and kumquat terrine

Tangy poached kumquats contrast perfectly with the sweet almond paste in this frozen terrine. Leftover kumquats keep in the fridge for a week, making a lovely topping for vanilla ice cream.

SERVES 6

350g/12oz/3 cups kumquats

115g/4oz/generous 1/2 cup caster (superfine) sugar

150ml/1/4 pint/2/3 cup water

2 egg yolks

10ml/2 tsp cornflour (cornstarch)

300ml/1/2 pint/11/4 cups full-cream (whole) milk

200g/7oz golden marzipan, grated

2.5ml/1/2 tsp almond extract

300ml/1/2 pint/11/4 cups whipping cream

1 Cut the kumquats in half and scoop out the seeds. Heat the sugar and water gently in a heavy pan until the sugar dissolves. Add the kumquats and cook gently for 10 minutes. Leave the syrup to cool.

2 Whisk the egg yolks, the cornflour and 60ml/4tbsp of the syrup in a bowl until smooth. Bring the milk to the boil, then pour it over the egg yolk mixture, whisking constantly. Return to the pan and cook gently for 2 minutes, stirring until thickened. Do not boil. Stir it into a bowl with the marzipan and almond extract. Cover with baking parchment and leave to cool.

3 Line a small terrine or loaf tin (pan) with clear film (plastic wrap). Set aside. Blend a third of the kumquats with 60ml/4 tbsp of the syrup until smooth.

4 Whip the cream until thickened and fold into the custard with the kumquat pulp. Freeze in the lined tin overnight. Transfer the tin to the fridge about 1 hour before serving to allow it to soften slightly. Invert on to a plate and remove the tin. Peel away the film and serve the terrine topped with the remaining kumquats.

Nutritional information per portion: Energy 477kcal/1992kJ; Protein 6g; Carbohydrate 52.8g, of which sugars 51.2g; Fat 28.2g, of which saturates 14.7g; Cholesterol 127mg; Calcium 146mg; Fibre 1.3g; Sodium 48mg.

Rhubarb and ginger wine torte

This luxurious torte combines rhubarb in a classic partnership with ginger. The result is a refreshingly tart flavour that's sure to go down well with those who prefer less sweet desserts.

SERVES 8

500g/1¼lb rhubarb, trimmed
115g/4oz/½ cup caster
    (superfine) sugar
30ml/2 tbsp water
200g/7oz/scant 1 cup cream cheese
150ml/¼ pint/⅔ cups double
    (heavy) cream
40g/1½oz/¼ cup preserved stem
    ginger, finely chopped
a few drops of pink food
    colouring (optional)
250ml/8fl oz/1 cup ginger wine
175g/6oz sponge fingers
fresh mint or lemon balm sprigs, dusted
    with icing (confectioners') sugar,
    to decorate

1 Chop the rhubarb roughly and cook gently in a covered pan with the sugar and water for 5–8 minutes until just tender. Process in a food processor or blender until smooth, then leave to cool.

2 Beat the cream cheese in a bowl until softened. Stir in the cream, rhubarb purée and ginger, then a little food colouring. Line a 900g/2lb/6-8 cup loaf tin (pan) with clear film (plastic wrap). Pour the mixture into a shallow container and freeze until firm.

3 Pour the ginger wine into a shallow dish. Spoon a thin layer of ice cream into the prepared tin. Dip the sponge fingers in the ginger wine, then lay them lengthways over the ice cream in a single layer. Trim to fit.

4 Spread another layer of ice cream over the sponge fingers. Repeat the process, adding two to three more layers and finishing with ice cream. Cover and freeze overnight. Transfer to the fridge 30 minutes before serving, to soften the torte slightly.

Nutritional information per portion: Energy 398kcal/1658kJ; Protein 3.9g; Carbohydrate 29.4g, of which sugars 25.2g; Fat 26.8g, of which saturates 16.2g; Cholesterol 100mg; Calcium 132mg; Fibre 1.2g; Sodium 111mg.

Iced Christmas torte

This exciting alternative to Christmas pudding doesn't have to be limited to the festive season. Packed with dried fruit and nuts, it's a treat for any special occasion.

SERVES 8–10

75g/3oz/³/₄ cup dried cranberries

75g/3oz/scant ¹/₂ cup pitted prunes

50g/2oz/¹/₃ cup sultanas (golden raisins)

175ml/6fl oz/³/₄ cup port

2 pieces preserved stem ginger,
    finely chopped

25g/1oz//2 tbsp unsalted (sweet) butter

45ml/3 tbsp light muscovado
    (brown) sugar

90g/3¹/₂ oz/scant 2 cups fresh
    white breadcrumbs

600ml/1 pint/2¹/₂ cups double
    (heavy) cream

30ml/2 tbsp icing (confectioners') sugar

5ml/1 tsp ground mixed (apple pie) spice

75g/3oz/³/₄ cup brazil nuts,
    finely chopped

sugared bay leaves and fresh cherries,
    to decorate

1 Quickly process the cranberries, prunes and sultanas in a food processor. Pour them into a bowl and add the port and ginger. Leave for 2 hours.

2 Melt the butter in a frying pan. Add the sugar and heat gently until the sugar dissolves. Pour in the breadcrumbs, stir lightly, then fry over a low heat for about 5 minutes until lightly coloured and turning crisp. Leave to cool.

3 Finely process the breadcrumbs in a food processor. Sprinkle a third into an 18cm/7in loose-based springform cake tin (pan) and freeze. Whip the cream, icing sugar and mixed spice until thick but not yet standing in peaks. Fold in the brazil nuts with the dried fruit mixture and any port that has not been absorbed.

4 Spread a third of the mixture over the frozen breadcrumb base. Sprinkle with another layer of the breadcrumbs. Repeat the layering, finishing with a layer of the cream mixture. Freeze the torte overnight. Make the sugared bay leaves, dipping the washed leaves first in beaten egg white, then sugar. Chill for about 1 hour before serving, decorated with bay leaves and fresh cherries.

Nutritional information per portion: Energy 504kcal/2098kJ; Protein 6.3g; Carbohydrate 38.4g, of which sugars 21g; Fat 36.4g, of which saturates 17.8g; Cholesterol 61mg; Calcium 92mg; Fibre 2.3g; Sodium 209mg.

Zabaglione ice cream torte

For lovers of zabaglione, the famous, whisked Italian dessert, this simple iced version is a must. Its taste and texture are just as good, and there's no last-minute whisking.

SERVES 10

175g/6oz amaretti
115g/4oz/½ cup ready-to-eat dried
 apricots, finely chopped
65g/2½oz/5 tbsp unsalted (sweet)
 butter, melted

FOR THE ICE CREAM
65g/2½oz/5 tbsp light muscovado
 (brown) sugar
75ml/5 tbsp water
5 egg yolks

250ml/8fl oz/1 cup double (heavy) cream
75ml/5 tbsp Madeira or cream sherry

FOR THE APRICOT COMPOTE
150g/5oz/generous ½ cup ready-to-eat
 dried apricots
25g/1oz/2 tbsp light muscovado
 (brown) sugar
150ml/¼ pint/⅔ cup water

1 Put the biscuits in a strong plastic bag and crush finely with a rolling pin. Tip into a bowl and stir in the apricots and melted butter until evenly combined. Using a dessertspoon, pack the mixture evenly on to the bottom and up the sides of a 24cm/9½in loose-based flan tin (pan) about 4cm/1½in deep. Chill.

2 In a small, heavy pan, heat the sugar and water, stirring until the sugar dissolves. Boil for 2 minutes without stirring. Bring a large pan of water to simmering point. Put the yolks in a heatproof bowl to fit over the pan without touching the water.

3 Off the heat, whisk the egg yolks until pale, then slowly whisk in the sugar syrup. Put the bowl over the pan of simmering water and continue to whisk for 10 minutes or until the mixture leaves a trail when the whisk is lifted. Remove the bowl from the heat and carry on whisking for a further 5 minutes or until the mixture is cold. In a separate bowl, whip the cream with the Madeira or sherry until it stands in peaks. Using a large metal spoon, fold the cream into the whisked mixture. Spoon it into the biscuit case, level the surface, cover and freeze overnight.

4 To make the compote, simmer the apricots and sugar in the water until the apricots are plump and the juices are syrupy, adding a little more water if necessary. Leave to cool. Serve the torte in slices with a little of the compote spooned over each portion.

Nutritional information per portion: Energy 333kcal/1387kJ; Protein 3.4g; Carbohydrate 25.8g, of which sugars 18.2g; Fat 23.9g, of which saturates 13.6g; Cholesterol 149mg; Calcium 60mg; Fibre 1g; Sodium 110mg.

Chocolate and brandied fig torte

This is a seriously rich torte for chocolate lovers. If, however, you are not keen on figs, you can easily use dried prunes, dates or apricots instead.

SERVES 8

250g/9oz/1½ cups dried figs
60ml/4 tbsp brandy
200g/7oz gingernut (gingersnap) biscuits
175g/6oz/¾ cup unsalted (sweet) butter, softened
150ml/¼ pint/⅔ cup milk

250g/9oz plain (semisweet) chocolate, broken into pieces
45ml/3 tbsp caster (superfine) sugar
unsweetened cocoa powder, for dusting
lightly whipped cream or crème fraîche, to serve

1 Chop the figs and put them into a bowl, pour over the brandy and leave for 2–3 hours until most of the brandy has been absorbed. Break the biscuits into large chunks, put them in a strong plastic bag and crush them with a rolling pin.

2 Melt half the butter and stir in the biscuit crumbs until combined. Pack on to the bottom and up the sides of a 20cm/8in loose-based flan tin (pan), which is about 3cm/1¼in deep. Chill.

3 Pour the milk into a pan, add the chocolate pieces and heat gently, stirring frequently, until the chocolate has melted and the mixture is smooth. Pour the chocolate mixture into a bowl and leave to cool.

4 In a separate bowl, beat the remaining butter with the caster sugar until the mixture is pale and creamy.

5 Add the chocolate mixture, whisking until it is well mixed. Fold in the figs, and any remaining brandy, and spoon the mixture into the biscuit case. Level the surface, cover and freeze overnight.

6 Transfer the torte to the fridge about 30 minutes before serving so that the filling softens slightly. Dust lightly with cocoa powder and serve in slices, with lightly whipped cream or crème fraîche.

Nutritional information per portion: Energy 539kcal/2257kJ; Protein 5g; Carbohydrate 63.9g, of which sugars 54.2g; Fat 29.7g, of which saturates 17.7g; Cholesterol 50mg; Calcium 172mg; Fibre 4.1g; Sodium 241mg.

Raspberry mousse gâteau

A lavish quantity of raspberries gives this gâteau its vibrant colour. It is best to make it at the height of summer, when raspberries are plentiful and full of flavour.

SERVES 8–10

2 eggs
50g/2oz/¼ cup caster (superfine) sugar
50g/2oz/½ cup plain (all-purpose) flour
30ml/2 tbsp unsweetened cocoa powder
600g/1lb 5oz/3½ cups raspberries

115g/4oz/1 cup icing (confectioners') sugar
60ml/4 tbsp whisky (optional)
300ml/½ pint/1¼ cups whipping cream
2 egg whites

1 Preheat the oven to 180°C/350°F/Gas 4. Grease and line a 23cm/9in springform cake tin (pan). Whisk the eggs and sugar in a heatproof bowl over a pan of gently simmering water until the whisk leaves a trail when lifted. Remove the bowl from the heat and continue to whisk the mixture for 2 minutes.

2 Sift the flour and unsweetened cocoa powder over the mixture and fold it in with a large metal spoon. Spoon the mixture into the tin and spread it gently to the edges. Bake for 12–15 minutes until just firm. Leave to cool, then remove the cake from the tin and place it on a wire rack. Wash and dry the tin.

3 Line the sides of the clean tin with a strip of baking parchment and carefully lower the cake back into it. Freeze until the raspberry filling is ready.

4 Set aside 200g/7oz/generous 1 cup of the raspberries. Put the remainder in a clean bowl, stir in the icing sugar, process to a purée in a food processor or blender. Strain the purée into a bowl, then stir in the whisky, if using.

5 Whip the cream to form soft peaks. Whisk the egg whites until they are stiff. Using a large metal spoon, fold the cream, then the egg whites into the raspberry purée.

6 Spread half the raspberry mixture over the cake. Scatter with the reserved raspberries. Spread the remaining raspberry mixture on top and level the surface. Cover and freeze the gâteau overnight.

7 Transfer the gâteau to the fridge at least 1 hour before serving. Remove it from the tin, place on a serving plate and serve in slices.

Nutritional information per portion: Energy 238kcal/996kJ; Protein 4.4g; Carbohydrate 25g, of which sugars 20.9g; Fat 14.1g, of which saturates 8.3g; Cholesterol 70mg; Calcium 58mg; Fibre 2g; Sodium 65mg.

Pistachio and nougat torte

Nougat, honey, pistachio nuts and rose water make a perfect blend of flavours in this quick and easy torte. Transfer to the fridge about an hour before serving.

SERVES 8

75g/3oz/³⁄₄ cup pistachio nuts
150g/5oz nougat
300ml/¹⁄₂ pint/1¹⁄₄ cups whipping cream
90ml/6 tbsp clear honey
30ml/2 tbsp rose water
250g/9oz/generous 1 cup fromage frais
   (low-fat cream cheese)
8 trifle sponges
icing (confectioners') sugar, for dusting
fresh raspberries, poached apricots or
   cherries, to serve (optional)

1 Soak the pistachio nuts in boiling water for 2 minutes. Drain thoroughly and rub between pieces of kitchen paper to remove the skins, then chop roughly. Cut the nougat into small pieces. Pour the cream into a bowl, add the honey and rose water and whip until it is just beginning to hold its shape.

2 Stir in the fromage frais, chopped pistachio nuts and nougat, and mix well. Slice the trifle sponges horizontally into three very thin layers.

3 Line a 15–17cm/6–6¹⁄₂in square loose-based cake tin (pan) with baking parchment or clear film (plastic wrap). Arrange a layer of sponges on the bottom; trim to fit. Pack with the filling, level and cover with the remaining sponges. Cover and freeze overnight.

4 To serve, invert the torte on to a serving plate and dust with icing sugar. Serve with raspberries, poached apricots or cherries, if you like.

Nutritional information per portion: Energy 462kcal/1929kJ; Protein 8.8g; Carbohydrate 46.7g, of which sugars 38.1g; Fat 28g, of which saturates 14.2g; Cholesterol 134mg; Calcium 119mg; Fibre 0.9g; Sodium 129mg.

Soft fruit and crushed meringue gâteau

This recipe takes five minutes to make but looks great and tastes as though a lot of preparation went into it. For perfect results, only use high-quality vanilla ice cream.

SERVES 6

400g/14oz/3¹/₂ cups mixed small strawberries, raspberries or redcurrants
30ml/2 tbsp icing (confectioners') sugar
750ml/1¹/₄ pints/3 cups Classic Vanilla ice cream
6 meringue nests (or 115g/4oz meringue)

1 Dampen a 900g/2lb loaf tin (pan) and line it with clear film (plastic wrap). If using strawberries, chop them into small pieces. Put them in a bowl and add the raspberries or redcurrants and icing sugar. Toss until the fruit is beginning to break up but do not let it become mushy.

2 Put the ice cream in a bowl and break it up with a fork. Then crumble the meringues into the bowl and add the soft fruit mixture.

3 Fold all the ingredients together until evenly combined and lightly marbled. Pack into the prepared tin and press down gently to level. Cover and freeze overnight. To serve, invert on to a plate and peel away the clear film. Serve in slices.

Nutritional information per portion: Energy 332kcal/1397kJ; Protein 6.1g; Carbohydrate 52.4g, of which sugars 51g; Fat 10.8g, of which saturates 7.6g; Cholesterol 30mg; Calcium 141mg; Fibre 0.7g; Sodium 102mg.

Rich chocolate mousse gâteau

Because this gâteau is heavily laced with liqueur, you can easily get away with using a sponge bought from a shop. The mousse is rich, so serve small portions only.

SERVES 12

400g/14oz moist chocolate sponge cake

75ml/5 tbsp Cointreau or other
   orange-flavoured liqueur

finely grated rind and juice of 1 orange

300g/11oz plain (semisweet) chocolate,
   broken into pieces

25g/1oz/¼ cup unsweetened cocoa powder

45ml/3 tbsp golden (light corn) syrup

3 eggs

300ml/½ pint/1¼ cups whipping cream

150ml/¼ pint/⅔ cup double (heavy)
   cream, lightly whipped

unsweetened cocoa powder, for dusting

1 Cut the cake into 5mm/¼in thick slices. Set a third aside, and use the remainder to make a case for the mousse. Line the bottom of a 23cm/9in springform or loose-based cake tin (pan) with cake, trimming to fit neatly, then use more for the sides, making a case about 4cm/1½ in deep.

2 Mix 30ml/2 tbsp of the liqueur with the orange juice and drizzle over the sponge case.

3 Place the chocolate, cocoa powder, syrup and remaining liqueur in a heatproof bowl over a pan of gently simmering water. Remove when the chocolate melts. Stir until smooth.

4 Whisk the eggs with the orange rind in a mixing bowl until they are thick and pale. Whip the whipping cream until it forms soft peaks.

5 Fold the chocolate mixture into the whisked eggs, using a large metal spoon, then fold in the cream. Scrape the mixture into the sponge case and level the surface.

6 Cover with the reserved chocolate cake, trimming the pieces to fit. Cover and freeze overnight.

7 Transfer the gâteau to the fridge 30 minutes before serving. Invert on to a plate, spread with the double cream and dust with the unsweetened cocoa powder.

Nutritional information per portion: Energy 488kcal/2032kJ; Protein 6g; Carbohydrate 37.4g, of which sugars 29.6g; Fat 34.4g, of which saturates 15.3g; Cholesterol 92mg; Calcium 61mg; Fibre 1.2g; Sodium 175mg.

Iced strawberry and lemon curd gâteau

Layer two favourite flavours in this fresh fruit gâteau, which is just perfect for summer entertaining and takes only minutes to assemble.

SERVES 8

115g/4oz/¹/₂ cup unsalted (sweet)
  butter, softened
115g/4oz/generous ¹/₂ cup caster
  (superfine) sugar
2 eggs
115g/4oz/1 cup self-raising (self-rising) flour
2.5ml/¹/₂ tsp baking powder

TO FINISH
500ml/17fl oz/2¹/₄ cups Simple Strawberry
  ice cream

300ml/¹/₂ pint/1¹/₄ cups double
  (heavy) cream
200g/7oz/scant 1 cup good quality
  lemon curd
30ml/2 tbsp lemon juice
500g/1¹/₄lb/5 cups strawberries, hulled
25g/1oz/2 tbsp caster (superfine) sugar
45ml/3 tbsp Cointreau or other
  orange-flavoured liqueur

1 Preheat the oven to 180°C/350°F/Gas 4. Grease and line a 23cm/9in round springform cake tin (pan). In a mixing bowl, beat the butter, sugar, eggs, flour and baking powder until creamy. Spoon into the prepared tin and bake until firm (about 20 minutes). Leave to cool for 5 minutes, then turn out on a wire rack. Cool completely. Wash and dry the cake tin, ready to use again.

2 Line the sides of the tin with non-stick baking parchment. Slice off the top of the cake where it has formed a crust. Fit the cake in the tin, cut-side down, and freeze for 10 minutes. Spread the strawberry ice cream evenly over the sponge and freeze until firm.

3 In a bowl, whip the cream into soft peaks, fold in the lemon curd and lemon juice, and spoon over the strawberry ice cream. Cover and freeze overnight. About 45 minutes before serving, blend half the strawberries, the sugar and liqueur to a purée. Decorate the frozen gâteau with thin strawberry slices and pour over the sauce.

Nutritional information per portion: Energy 653kcal/2725kJ; Protein 6.5g; Carbohydrate 66.8g, of which sugars 49.9g; Fat 40.2g, of which saturates 24.6g; Cholesterol 150mg; Calcium 164mg; Fibre 1.2g; Sodium 224mg.

Zucotto

An Italian-style dessert with a rich ricotta, fruit, chocolate and nut filling, zucotto is encased in a moist, chocolate- and liqueur-flavoured sponge.

SERVES 8

3 eggs
75g/3oz/6 tbsp caster (superfine) sugar
75g/3oz/²/₃ cup plain (all-purpose) flour
25g/1oz/¹/₄ cup unsweetened cocoa powder
90ml/6 tbsp Kirsch
250g/9oz/generous 1 cup ricotta cheese
50g/2oz/¹/₂ cup icing (confectioners') sugar
50g/2oz plain (semisweet) chocolate, finely chopped

50g/2oz/¹/₂ cup blanched almonds, chopped and toasted
75g/3oz/scant ¹/₂ cup natural glacé (candied) cherries, quartered
2 pieces preserved stem ginger, finely chopped
150ml/¹/₄ pint/²/₃ cup double (heavy) cream
unsweetened cocoa powder, for dusting

1 Heat the oven to 180°C/350°F/Gas 4. Grease and line a 23cm/9in cake tin (pan). Whisk the eggs and sugar in a heatproof bowl over a pan of simmering water until the whisk leaves a trail. Remove the bowl from the heat and continue to whisk the mixture for 2 minutes.

2 Fold the flour and cocoa into the bowl with a large metal spoon. Spoon the mixture into the prepared tin and bake for 20 minutes until firm. Leave to cool.

3 Cut the cake horizontally into three layers. Set aside 30ml/2 tbsp of the Kirsch and drizzle the remainder over the layers. Beat the ricotta in a bowl until soft; beat in the icing sugar, chocolate, almonds, cherries, ginger and reserved kirsch. Pour the cream into a separate bowl, whip lightly and fold into the ricotta mixture. Chill. Cut a 20cm/8in circle from one sponge layer and set it aside.

4 Cut the remaining sponge cake to fit the bottom of a 2.8–3.4 litre/5–6 pint/12¹/₂–15 cup freezerproof mixing bowl. Cut more sponge for the sides of the bowl, fitting them together to cover one third of the way up. Spoon the ricotta filling into the bowl to the height of the sponge, and level. Fit the reserved circle of sponge on top of the filling. Trim off excess sponge around the edges. Cover and freeze overnight. Transfer to the fridge 45 minutes before serving to let the filling soften slightly. Invert on to a serving plate and peel away the clear film (plastic wrap). Dust with the cocoa powder and serve in slices.

Nutritional information per portion: Energy 391kcal/1631kJ; Protein 8.7g; Carbohydrate 33.8g, of which sugars 26.1g; Fat 22.7g, of which saturates 11.4g; Cholesterol 111mg; Calcium 66mg; Fibre 1.3g; Sodium 64mg.

Iced lime cheesecake

*This cheesecake has a deliciously tangy, sweet flavour, and needs no gelatine to set the filling.
It is not difficult to prepare and looks pleasantly summery with its citrus decoration.*

SERVES 10

175g/6oz almond biscuits
65g/2¹/₂oz/5 tbsp unsalted
   (sweet) butter
rind and juice of 5 limes, plus 3 limes
   peeled and finely sliced, to decorate
115g/4oz/¹/₂ cup caster
   (superfine) sugar
90ml/6 tbsp water
200g/7oz/scant 1 cup cottage cheese
250g/9oz/generous 1 cup mascarpone
300ml/¹/₂ pint/1¹/₄ cups double
   (heavy) cream

1 Lightly grease the sides of a 20cm/8in springform tin (pan) and line with baking parchment. Crush the almond biscuits in a strong plastic bag with a rolling pin. Evenly combine the melted butter and biscuits in a small pan. Then, tightly pack the mixture into the tin with the back of a spoon and freeze.

2 Finely grate the rind and squeeze the juice of 5 limes. Heat the sugar and water in a small pan, stirring until the sugar dissolves. Then boil for 2 minutes without stirring, remove the syrup from the heat, stir in the lime juice and rind, and leave to cool.

3 Press the cottage cheese through a sieve (strainer) into a bowl. Beat in the mascarpone, then the lime syrup. Lightly whip the cream and fold into the cheese mixture. Pour into a shallow container and freeze until thick. Then decorate the sides of the tin with thin slices of peeled lime. Evenly pour the cheese mixture over the biscuit base. Cover and freeze overnight.

4 Transfer to a serving plate in the fridge 1 hour before serving.

Nutritional information per portion: Energy 385kcal/1602kJ; Protein 6.4g; Carbohydrate 28g, of which sugars 20.5g; Fat 28.1g, of which saturates 17.2g; Cholesterol 69mg; Calcium 71mg; Fibre 0.3g; Sodium 165mg.

Iced butterscotch tart

This dessert has a delicious butterscotch flavour. Remember to chill the evaporated milk for a couple of hours before you are ready to make the filling.

SERVES 8

FOR THE CASE
90g/3¹/₂oz ginger nut (gingersnap) biscuits
75g/3oz/³/₄ cup ground hazelnuts, toasted
50g/2oz/¹/₄ cup unsalted (sweet) butter, melted

FOR THE FILLING
300ml/¹/₂ pint/1¹/₄ cups evaporated (unsweetened condensed) milk, chilled
150g/5oz/²/₃ cup dark muscovado (molasses) sugar
1 egg white
150ml/¹/₄ pint/²/₃ cup double (heavy) cream
chopped toasted hazelnuts and demerara (raw) sugar, to decorate

1 Use a rolling pin to crush the biscuits in a strong plastic bag. Tip them into a bowl and add the toasted nuts and the butter. Mix until evenly combined.

2 Press on to the base and slightly up the sides of a 24cm/9¹/₂in loose-based flan tin (pan) or freezerproof dish that is about 4cm/1¹/₂in deep.

3 Whisk the evaporated milk and sugar in a large bowl until the mixture is pale and thick and leaves a thick trail when the whisk is lifted. In a separate, clean bowl, whisk the egg white until stiff. Whip the double cream separately until it forms soft peaks.

4 Using a large metal spoon, fold first the cream and then the egg white into the whisked evaporated milk and sugar. Pour the mixture into the biscuit case. Cover and freeze overnight.

5 To serve, sprinkle the tart with hazelnuts and demerara sugar, and cut into thin wedges.

Nutritional information per portion: Energy 365kcal/1523kJ; Protein 5.7g; Carbohydrate 33.3g, of which sugars 28.2g; Fat 24.2g, of which saturates 11.6g; Cholesterol 45mg; Calcium 146mg; Fibre 0.8g; Sodium 132mg.

Iced desserts & hot ice cream puddings

Whether scooped into glasses and bathed in a sweet glossy sauce, or encased in chocolate, there is an iced dessert here for every occasion. Or you can enjoy the soft, melting texture of ice cream as it seeps into a deliciously warm pastry or mingles with the juices of a hot fruit compote, bringing out the flavours of both.

White chocolate castles

Chocolate cases have a wide variety of uses. They can be frozen with iced mousses or used for setting other desserts. In this recipe, they are filled with ice cream and succulent blueberries.

SERVES 6

225g/8oz white chocolate, broken into pieces
250ml/8fl oz/1 cup Double White Chocolate ice cream
250ml/8fl oz/1 cup Classic Dark Chocolate ice cream
115g/4oz/1 cup blueberries
unsweetened cocoa powder or icing (confectioners') sugar for dusting

1 Simmer the white chocolate in a heatproof bowl over a pan of water until melted. Line a baking sheet with baking parchment. Cut out six 30 x 13cm/12 x 5in strips of baking parchment, then fold each in half lengthways.

2 Stand a 7.5cm/3in pastry cutter on the baking sheet. Roll one strip of paper into a tube and fit inside the cutter with the folded edge on the base paper. Tape the edges together.

3 Remove the cutter and shape more paper collars in the same way, leaving the pastry cutter in place around the final collar.

4 Spoon a little of the melted chocolate into the base of the collar supported by the cutter. With a teaspoon, spread the chocolate over the base and up the sides of the collar, making the top edge uneven. Carefully lift away the cutter. Make five more cases in the same way, leaving them to set in the fridge.

5 Carefully peel away the paper from the sides of the chocolate cases then lift the cases off the base. Transfer to serving plates.

6 Using a large melon baller or teaspoon, scoop the white and dark chocolate ice creams into the cases and decorate with the fruit. Dust with cocoa powder or icing sugar and serve at once.

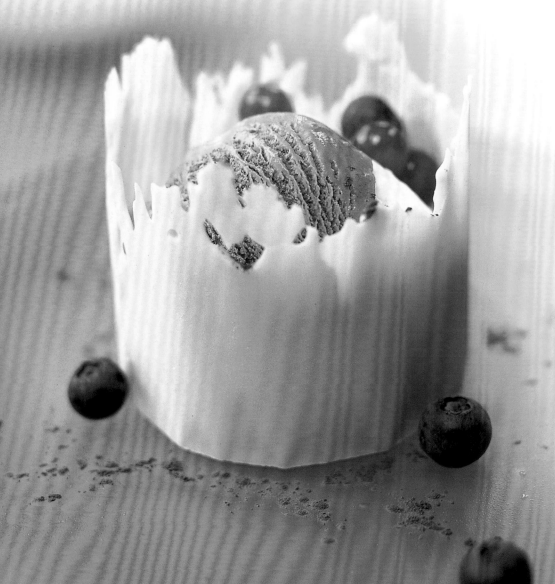

Nutritional information per portion: Energy 351kcal/1463kJ; Protein 6g; Carbohydrate 34.3g, of which sugars 34.2g; Fat 22g, of which saturates 13.1g; Cholesterol 150mg; Calcium 182mg; Fibre 1.2g; Sodium 84mg.

Sorbet in an ice bowl

Nothing sets off a sorbet quite so effectively as an ice bowl inlaid with fresh flowers and leaves. Easy to make, inexpensive and stunning, ice bowls grace any special occasion.

SERVES 8–10

ice cubes
cold water
selection of fresh edible flowers
    and leaves
18–20 scoops of sorbet, to serve

1 Place some ice cubes in the base of a 3.5 litre/6 pint/15 cup clear plastic or glass freezerproof bowl. Tuck some flowers and leaves around the ice. Position a smaller bowl so that it rests on the ice cubes, leaving an even space between the two bowls.

2 Pour cold water into the space between the bowls until the water level starts to come up the sides. Freeze for 2–3 hours until frozen.

3 Tuck more flowers and leaves between the two bowls, mixing the flowers and leaves so that they look attractive through the sides of the larger bowl.

4 Place some kitchen weights or food cans in the central bowl to stop it from rising, then fill the space between the bowls to the rim with more water. Freeze overnight until firm.

5 Release the inner bowl by pouring in boiling water almost to the top. Tip out the water and lift away the inner bowl. Repeat the process if it doesn't come free instantly.

6 To remove the outer bowl, dip it quickly in a large bowl of very hot water until the ice bowl loosens. Return the ice bowl to the freezer.

7 Shortly before serving, scoop the sorbet into the bowl. Return to the freezer until ready to serve.

Nutritional information per portion: Energy 73kcal/308kJ; Protein 0.2g; Carbohydrate 18.6g, of which sugars 17.5g; Fat 0.2g, of which saturates 0g; Cholesterol 0mg; Calcium 6mg; Fibre 0g; Sodium 8mg.

Iced raspberry and almond trifle

This delicious combination of almondy sponge, sherried fruit, ice cream and mascarpone topping is sheer indulgence for trifle lovers. The sponge and topping can be made a day in advance and the assembled trifle will sit happily in the fridge for an hour before serving.

SERVES 8–10

FOR THE SPONGE

115g/4oz/1/2 cup unsalted (sweet) butter, softened

115g/4oz/1/2 cup light muscovado (brown) sugar

2 eggs

75g/3oz/2/3 cup self-raising (self-rising) flour

2.5ml/1/2 tsp baking powder

115g/4oz/1 cup ground almonds

5ml/1 tsp almond extract

15ml/1 tbsp milk

TO FINISH

300g/11oz/scant 2 cups raspberries

50g/2oz/1/2 cup flaked (sliced) almonds, toasted

90ml/6 tbsp fresh orange juice

200ml/7fl oz/scant 1 cup medium sherry

500g/11/4lb/21/2 cups mascarpone

150g/5oz/2/3 cup Greek (strained plain) yogurt

30ml/2 tbsp icing (confectioners') sugar

250ml/8fl oz/1 cup Classic Vanilla ice cream

250ml/8fl oz/1 cup Raspberry Sorbet

1 Preheat the oven to 180°C/350°F/Gas 4. Grease and line a 20cm/8in round cake tin (pan). Beat the butter, sugar, eggs, flour, baking powder, almonds and almond extract in a large bowl with an electric whisk for 2 minutes until creamy. Stir in the milk.

2 Spoon the mixture into the tin, level the surface and bake for about 30 minutes or until just firm in the centre. Leave to cool on a wire rack.

3 Cut the sponge into chunky pieces and place these in the base of a 1.75 litre/3 pint/71/2 cup glass serving dish. Scatter with half the raspberries and flaked almonds. Mix the orange juice with 90ml/6 tbsp of the sherry.

4 Spoon over the orange and sherry mixture. Beat the mascarpone in a bowl with the yogurt, icing sugar and remaining sherry. Put the trifle dish and the mascarpone in the fridge until you are ready to assemble the trifle.

5 Scoop the ice cream and sorbet into the trifle dish. Reserve a few of the remaining raspberries and almonds for decoration, then scatter the rest over the ice cream. Spoon over the mascarpone mixture and scatter with the reserved raspberries and almonds. Chill the trifle for up to 1 hour.

Nutritional information per portion: Energy 330kcal/1382kJ; Protein 5g; Carbohydrate 35.9g, of which sugars 29.1g; Fat 17.7g, of which saturates 9.9g; Cholesterol 90mg; Calcium 102mg; Fibre 1.1g; Sodium 59mg.

Gooseberry and elderflower sorbet

A classic combination that makes a really refreshing sorbet. Try making it in summer, as a stunning finale to an alfresco meal, or serve it to follow a hearty winter's stew.

SERVES 6

150g/5oz/²/₃ cup caster (superfine) sugar
175ml/6fl oz/³/₄ cup water
10 elderflower heads, plus extra to decorate
500g/1¼lb/4 cups gooseberries

200ml/7fl oz/scant 1 cup apple juice
dash of green food colouring (optional)
a little beaten egg white and caster sugar,
    to decorate

1 Put 30ml/2 tbsp of the sugar in a pan with 30ml/2 tbsp of the water. Set aside. Mix the remaining sugar and water in a separate, heavy pan. Heat gently, stirring occasionally, until the sugar has dissolved. Bring to the boil and boil for 1 minute, without stirring, to make a syrup.

2 Remove from the heat and add the elderflower heads, pressing them into the syrup with a wooden spoon. Leave to infuse for about 1 hour.

3 Strain the elderflower syrup through a sieve (strainer) placed over a bowl. Set the strained syrup aside. Add the gooseberries to the pan containing the reserved sugar and water. Cover and cook very gently for about 5 minutes until the gooseberries have softened.

4 Transfer to a food processor and add the apple juice. Process until smooth, then strain into a bowl. Leave to cool. Stir in the reserved elderflower syrup and green food colouring. Chill until very cold.

5 Pour the mixture into a shallow container and freeze until thick, preferably overnight.

6 To decorate the glasses, put a little egg white in a shallow bowl and a thin layer of caster sugar on a flat plate. Dip the rim of each glass in the egg white, then the sugar to coat evenly. Leave to dry. Scoop the sorbet carefully into the glasses, decorate with elderflowers and serve.

Nutritional information per portion: Energy 127kcal/542kJ; Protein 1.1g; Carbohydrate 31.9g, of which sugars 31.9g; Fat 0.4g, of which saturates 0g; Cholesterol 0mg; Calcium 39mg; Fibre 2g; Sodium 4mg.

Cranberry sorbet in lace pancakes

Pretty lace pancakes make a really stunning presentation for sorbets and ice creams. The sweet yet tangy cranberry sorbet can be made using fresh or frozen cranberries.

SERVES 6

500g/1¼lb/5 cups cranberries
225g/8oz/1 cup caster (superfine) sugar
300ml/½ pint/1¼ cups orange juice
60ml/4 tbsp Cointreau or other
    orange-flavoured liqueur
icing (confectioners') sugar, for dusting
extra cranberries and lightly whipped cream,
    to serve

FOR THE PANCAKES

50g/2oz/½ cup plain (all-purpose) flour
2.5ml/½ tsp ground ginger
1 egg
15ml/1 tbsp caster (superfine) sugar
120ml/4fl oz/½ cup milk
a little oil, for frying

1 Gently heat the cranberries, sugar and orange juice in a pan until the sugar dissolves. Cover and cook gently for 5–8 minutes more. Leave to cool.

2 Process in a food processor until smooth and press through a sieve (strainer) over a bowl. Stir the liqueur into the juice. Chill well. Pour the mixture into a shallow container and freeze for 3–4 hours, beating twice. Freeze again overnight.

3 In a bowl, whisk the flour, ginger, egg, sugar and a little milk to a smooth batter, gradually adding the remaining milk. Heat a little oil in a small frying pan or crêpe pan. Pour off the excess oil and remove the pan from the heat.

4 With a large spoon, drizzle a little of the batter over the bottom of the hot pan, creating a lacy effect. (The pancake should be about 14cm/5½in in diameter.) Return to the heat and cook gently until the lacy pancake is golden on the underside.

5 Carefully turn it over, and cook for 1 minute more. Slide on to a plate and leave to cool. Make 5 more pancakes in the same way, lightly oiling the pan each time.

6 To serve, lay a pancake on a serving plate, underside upwards. Arrange several small scoops of the sorbet on one side of the pancake. Fold over and dust generously with icing sugar. Scatter with extra cranberries. Serve with whipped cream.

Nutritional information per portion: Energy 326kcal/1381kJ; Protein 3.2g; Carbohydrate 61g, of which sugars 54.7g; Fat 7g, of which saturates 1.1g; Cholesterol 33mg; Calcium 70mg; Fibre 1.6g; Sodium 30mg.

Chocolate teardrops with cherry sauce

These sensational chocolate cases are surprisingly easy to make. Once filled, they freeze well, making them the perfect choice for a special occasion dessert.

SERVES 6

90g/3$\frac{1}{2}$oz plain (semisweet) chocolate, broken into pieces
115g/4oz amaretti
300ml/$\frac{1}{2}$ pint/1$\frac{1}{4}$ cups whipping cream
2.5ml/$\frac{1}{2}$ tsp almond extract
30ml/2 tbsp icing (confectioners') sugar
6 pairs of fresh cherries, to decorate

FOR THE SAUCE

2.5ml/$\frac{1}{2}$ tsp cornflour (cornstarch)
75ml/5 tbsp water
225g/8oz/2 cups fresh cherries, pitted and halved
45ml/3 tbsp caster (superfine) sugar
10ml/2 tsp lemon juice
45ml/3 tbsp gin

1 Cut out six perspex strips, each measuring 27 x 3cm/10$\frac{1}{2}$ x 1$\frac{1}{4}$in. Simmer the chocolate in a heatproof bowl over a pan of water until melted. Remove from the heat and leave for 5 minutes. Line a baking sheet with baking parchment.

2 Coat the underside of a perspex strip by dipping it in the chocolate, apart from 1cm/$\frac{1}{2}$in at each end. Keep the other side uncoated.

3 Bring the ends of the strip together, with the coated side on the inside. Hold the ends with a paper clip, then put on the baking sheet to set. Make five more shapes in the same way. Chill until set.

4 Crush the amaretti in a plastic bag with a rolling pin. Whip the cream, almond extract and icing sugar in a bowl until thick but soft. Fold in the biscuits. Fill the chocolate cases up to the rim.

5 Tap the baking sheet gently on the work surface to level the filling. Freeze the filled chocolate cases for 3 hours or overnight.

6 In a pan, stir the cornflour and a little water into a paste. Stir in the remaining water, cherries, sugar and lemon juice. Bring to the boil, stirring until thickened. Remove from the heat and leave to cool. Stir in the gin.

7 Remove the paper clips and peel off the perspex. Transfer the shapes to individual dessert plates. Spoon a little sauce on to each plate and decorate with pairs of cherries.

Nutritional information per portion: Energy 441kcal/1839kJ; Protein 3.3g; Carbohydrate 45g, of which sugars 36.1g; Fat 26.9g, of which saturates 16.3g; Cholesterol 53mg; Calcium 72mg; Fibre 1.1g; Sodium 78mg.

Chocolate millefeuille slice

This stunning dessert can be prepared days in advance, ready to impress dinner guests. Simply transfer it to the fridge about 30 minutes before serving so that it's easier to slice.

SERVES 8

4 egg yolks
10ml/2 tsp cornflour (cornstarch)
300ml/¹⁄₂ pint/1¹⁄₄ cups milk
175ml/6fl oz/³⁄₄ cup maple syrup
250ml/8fl oz/1 cup crème fraîche
115g/4oz/1 cup pecan nuts, chopped

TO FINISH
200g/7oz plain (semi-sweet) chocolate
300ml/¹⁄₂ pint/1¹⁄₄ cups
    double (heavy) cream
45ml/3 tbsp icing (confectioners') sugar
30ml/2 tbsp brandy (optional)
lightly toasted pecan nuts

1 In a bowl, whisk the egg yolks, cornflour and a little milk until smooth. Pour the remaining milk into a pan, bring to the boil, then pour over the yolk mixture, stirring.

2 Return to the pan and stir in the maple syrup. Cook gently, stirring until thick and smooth. Do not boil. Pour into a bowl and cover closely with baking parchment to prevent a skin forming. Leave to cool.

3 Stir the crème fraîche into the cold custard, pour into a shallow container and freeze for 3–4 hours, beating twice as the mixture thickens. Then add the chopped pecan nuts and freeze once more overnight.

4 Melt 150g/5oz of the chocolate (in pieces) in a bowl over a pan of simmering water. On baking parchment, draw four rectangles, each measuring 19 x 12cm/7¹⁄₂ x 4¹⁄₂ in. Evenly spoon melted chocolate on to each rectangle and leave to set.

5 Pare thin curls from the remaining chocolate. Whip the cream, icing sugar and brandy into soft peaks. Peel the paper from one chocolate rectangle and place it on a flat freezerproof serving plate. Spread a third of the whipped cream on the chocolate, almost to the edges.

6 With a large spoon, shape and lay small scoops of ice cream over the cream. Cover with a second chocolate rectangle. Repeat the layering, finishing with chocolate. Scatter with toasted pecan nuts and chocolate curls. Freeze until firm.

Nutritional information per portion: Energy 667kcal/ 2772kJ; Protein 6.7g; Carbohydrate 43.3g, of which sugars 42.6g; Fat 53.1g, of which saturates 27.2g; Cholesterol 191mg; Calcium 117mg; Fibre 1.3g; Sodium 99mg.

Hazelnut cones with vanilla ice cream and hazelnut caramel sauce

These hazelnut biscuit cones taste delicious and keep well in an airtight container for several days. However, should they start to soften, pop them into a moderate oven for a minute or two.

SERVES 8

90g/3½oz/scant 1 cup ground hazelnuts
50g/2oz/½ cup plain (all-purpose) flour
50g/2oz/½ cup caster (superfine) sugar
2 eggs, lightly beaten
5ml/1 tsp natural vanilla extract
15ml/1 tbsp milk

FOR THE SAUCE

75g/3oz/6 tbsp caster (superfine) sugar
120ml/4floz/½ cup water
50g/2oz/½ cup hazelnuts, lightly toasted and
    roughly chopped
15ml/1 tbsp lemon juice
25g/1oz/2 tbsp unsalted (sweet) butter
about 500ml/17fl oz/2¼ cups Classic Vanilla ice cream

1 Preheat the oven to 180°C/350°F/Gas 4. Line a baking sheet with baking parchment. Mix the ground hazelnuts, flour and sugar in a bowl. Add the eggs, vanilla extract and milk and mix to a smooth paste.

2 Spoon one shallow tablespoonful of the mixture on to one end of the baking sheet and a second at the opposite end. With a metal spatula, evenly spread each spoonful to a circle about 13cm/5in in diameter. Bake the biscuits for about 5 minutes until they start to turn pale gold around the edges.

3 Quickly, lift a biscuit from the paper and turn it over. Wrap it around a cream horn mould. Repeat with the other biscuit. As soon as the biscuits are brittle, ease the cones away from the moulds. Make eight cones in all.

4 Heat the sugar and 60ml/4floz of the water in a small, heavy pan until the sugar has dissolved. Then boil rapidly, without stirring, until the caramel is a deep golden colour. Immerse the base of the pan in cold water to prevent further cooking. Add the remaining half of water, standing back in case the syrup splutters. Add the hazelnuts, lemon juice and butter to the pan and cook gently until the sauce is smooth and glossy. Pour it into a small jug.

5 Scoop the vanilla ice cream into the hazelnut cones, pour over a little sauce and serve immediately.

Nutritional information per portion: Energy 352kcal/1473kJ; Protein 7.3g; Carbohydrate 37.9g, of which sugars 30.7g; Fat 20.1g, of which saturates 5.4g; Cholesterol 59mg; Calcium 137mg; Fibre 1.3g; Sodium 76mg.

Pear and gingerbread sundaes

The best sundaes do not consist solely of ice cream but of a feast of melting flavours. Poach the pears and chill them well in advance, and you can assemble this dessert in minutes.

SERVES 4

65g/2½oz/⅓ cup light muscovado (brown) sugar

90ml/6 tbsp water

30ml/2 tbsp lemon juice

40g/1½oz/⅓ cup sultanas (golden raisins) or raisins

1.5ml/¼ tsp mixed (apple pie) spice

4 small pears

150g/5oz moist gingerbread or ginger cake

250ml/8fl oz/1 cup Classic Vanilla ice cream

1 Heat the sugar and water in a heavy pan until the sugar has dissolved. Add the lemon juice, sultanas or raisins and spice. Peel, quarter and core the pears and add them to the pan.

2 Cover and simmer very gently for 5–10 minutes until just tender. Then cool the pears in the syrup. Lift them out of the syrup and put them in a bowl. Pour the syrup into a jug. Chill both.

3 Cut the gingerbread or ginger cake into four pieces and arrange in four serving glasses. Divide the pears among the glasses, then pile ice cream in the centre of each portion. Pour a little of the syrup over each sundae and serve.

Nutritional information per portion: Energy 404kcal/1706kJ; Protein 5.2g; Carbohydrate 75.6g, of which sugars 63.7g; Fat 10.3g, of which saturates 3.8g; Cholesterol 15mg; Calcium 125mg; Fibre 4g; Sodium 120mg.

Coconut ice cream with mango sauce

Halved coconut shells make impressive serving containers for this rich, delicious ice cream. You'll need three coconuts to get six serving cups and enough trimmings.

SERVES 6

4 egg yolks
115g/4oz/½ cup caster
  (superfine) sugar
15ml/1 tbsp cornflour (cornstarch)
5ml/1 tsp almond extract
600ml/1 pint/2½ cups milk
150g/5oz/1½ cups freshly
  grated coconut
300ml/½ pint/1¼ cups whipping cream

FOR THE SAUCE

1 large ripe mango
30ml/2 tbsp caster (superfine) sugar
15ml/1 tbsp lemon juice
60ml/4 tbsp fresh orange juice

1 Beat the egg yolks, sugar, cornflour, almond extract and a little of the milk until combined. Process the coconut in a food processor with 300ml/½ pint/1¼ cups of the remaining milk until fairly smooth.

2 Stir together the rest of the milk and the fresh coconut milk in a heavy pan. Bring almost to the boil. Slowly pour the milk over the egg yolks whisking constantly. Return to the pan, cooking gently and stirring until thickened. Pour into a bowl, cover with baking parchment and leave to cool.

3 Whip the cream and fold into the cooled custard. Freeze in a container for 3–4 hours, beating twice as it thickens. Freeze again overnight.

4 In a food processor or blender, blend the mango flesh, sugar, lemon juice and orange juice until smooth. Pour into a small jug and chill. Scoop the ice cream into the coconut shells, add the sauce and serve immediately.

Nutritional information per portion: Energy 566kcal/2358kJ; Protein 8.2g; Carbohydrate 39.8g, of which sugars 37.4g; Fat 42.8g, of which saturates 29.6g; Cholesterol 193mg; Calcium 188mg; Fibre 0.7g; Sodium 73mg.

Ice cream with sweet pine nut sauce

The delicious combination of lightly toasted pine nuts, tangy lemon and butter makes an easy sauce that is just perfect for enlivening vanilla ice cream and lemon sorbet.

SERVES 4

75g/2½oz/5 tbsp pine nuts
25g/1oz/2tbsp unsalted (sweet) butter
30ml/2 tbsp clear honey
30ml/2 tbsp light muscovado
   (brown) sugar
pared rind and juice of 1 lemon
250ml/8 fl oz/1 cup Lemon Sorbet
250ml/8 fl oz/1 cup Classic Vanilla
   ice cream

1 Toast the pine nuts lightly, then chop them roughly. Melt the butter in a small, heavy pan with the honey and sugar. Remove from the heat and stir in the lemon rind and juice.

2 Stir in the chopped pine nuts. Pour the sauce into a small jug. Leave to cool until ready to serve.

3 To serve, alternate small scoops of the lemon sorbet and the vanilla ice cream in four tall serving glasses. Generously spoon the pine nut sauce over the ices and serve immediately.

COOK'S TIP
The sauce will be very thin while it is still warm, but it becomes thicker as it cools. It is best served before it is quite cold.

Nutritional information per portion: Energy 419kcal/1756kJ; Protein 5.6g; Carbohydrate 48.1g, of which sugars 47.4g; Fat 23.4g, of which saturates 7.9g; Cholesterol 29mg; Calcium 71mg; Fibre 0.4g; Sodium 88mg.

Iced coffee cups

Small, sturdy coffee cups make attractive containers for this richly flavoured ice cream. Alternatively, use ramekins or other small freezerproof dishes.

SERVES 6–8

150ml/¹/₄ pint/²/₃ cup water

75ml/5 tbsp ground espresso
   coffee beans

5ml/1 tsp cornflour (cornstarch)

4 egg yolks

65g/2¹/₂oz/5 tbsp light muscovado
   (brown) sugar

300ml/¹/₂ pint/1¹/₄ cups whipping cream

30ml/2 tbsp Tia Maria or Kahlúa liqueur

lightly whipped cream and drinking
   chocolate powder, to decorate

1 Pour the water into a small pan and stir in the ground coffee. Bring to the boil, remove from the heat and leave to infuse for 15 minutes. Strain through a muslin-lined (cheesecloth) sieve (strainer) held over a bowl.

2 Spoon the cornflour into a small, heavy pan. Stir in a little of the hot coffee, then the remaining coffee, egg yolks and sugar. Cook over a gentle heat, stirring until thickened. Do not boil or the mixture may curdle. Scrape into a bowl, cover closely with baking parchment and leave to cool.

3 Whip the cream with the liqueur and cooled coffee mixture into soft peaks.

4 Spoon the mixture into the coffee cups, tapping them gently to level the surface. Freeze for at least 3 hours.

5 Put the coffee cups in the fridge about 30 minutes before serving. Top with swirls of lightly whipped cream and dust with drinking chocolate powder.

Nutritional information per portion: Energy 220kcal/911kJ; Protein 2.2g; Carbohydrate 10.9g, of which sugars 10.4g; Fat 18.4g, of which saturates 10.3g; Cholesterol 140mg; Calcium 39mg; Fibre 0g; Sodium 18mg.

Chocolate ice cream in florentine baskets

A similar mixture to that used to make florentines is perfect for shaping fluted baskets to hold scoops of ice cream. For convenience, make them a couple of days in advance.

SERVES 8

115g/4oz/¹/₂ cup unsalted (sweet) butter, plus extra
    for greasing
50g/2oz/¹/₄ cup caster (superfine) sugar
90ml/6 tbsp golden (light corn) syrup
90g/3¹/₂oz/scant 1 cup plain (all-purpose) flour
50g/2oz/¹/₂ cup flaked (sliced) almonds

50g/2oz/¹/₄ cup glacé (candied) cherries,
    finely chopped
25g/1oz/3 tbsp raisins, chopped
15ml/1 tbsp preserved stem ginger, finely chopped
90g/3¹/₂oz plain (semisweet) chocolate, in pieces
about 750ml/1¹/₄ pints/3 cups Classic Dark Chocolate
    ice cream

1 Preheat the oven to 190°C/375°F/Gas 5. Line two large baking sheets with lightly greased baking parchment. In a small, heavy pan, heat the butter until it has melted and add the sugar and golden syrup. Off the heat, stir in the flour, almonds, cherries, raisins and ginger.

2 Place a shallow tablespoonful of the mixture at either end of a baking sheet, then spread each spoonful to a 13cm/5in round, using the back of the spoon.

3 Bake for about 5 minutes until each round has spread even more and looks lacy and deep golden. Spread more circles on the second baking sheet ready to put in the oven. Have ready several metal dariole moulds for shaping the baskets.

4 Leave the biscuits on the baking sheet for about 2 minutes to firm up slightly. Working quickly, lift one biscuit on a metal spatula and lay it over an upturned dariole mould. Gently shape the biscuit into flutes around the sides of the mould. Shape the other biscuit around a mould in the same way.

5 Leave the biscuits in place for about 2 minutes until cool, then carefully lift the baskets away from the dariole moulds. Cook and shape the remaining biscuit mixture in the same way until you have eight baskets in total.

6 Melt the chocolate in a heatproof bowl over a pan of gently simmering water. Carefully dip the edges of the baskets in the melted chocolate and place on individual dessert plates. Scoop the chocolate ice cream into the baskets to serve.

Nutritional information per portion: Energy 525kcal/2191kJ; Protein 6.8g; Carbohydrate 53.9g, of which sugars 45g; Fat 32.8g, of which saturates 18.2g; Cholesterol 31mg; Calcium 141mg; Fibre 1.2g; Sodium 180mg.

Fig, port and clementine sundaes

The delightful, warming, aromatic flavours of figs, cinnamon, clementines and port never fail to conjure up comforting images of winter, warm fires and hearty meals.

SERVES 6

6 clementines
30ml/2 tbsp clear honey
1 cinnamon stick, halved
15ml/1 tbsp light muscovado
    (brown) sugar
60ml/4 tbsp port
6 fresh figs
approx 500ml/17fl oz/2¹/₄ cups
    Orange Sorbet

1 Finely grate the rind from two clementines and put it in a small, heavy pan. Using a small, sharp knife cut the peel away from all the clementines, then slice the flesh thinly. Add the honey, cinnamon, sugar and port to the clementine rind. Heat gently until the sugar has dissolved, to make a syrup.

2 Put the clementine slices in a heatproof bowl and pour over the syrup. Cool completely, then chill.

3 Slice the figs thinly and add to the clementines and syrup, tossing together gently. Leave for 10 minutes, then discard the cinnamon stick.

4 Arrange half the fig and clementine slices around the sides of six serving glasses. Half fill the glasses with scoops of sorbet. Arrange the remaining fruit slices around the sides of the glasses, then pile more sorbet into the centre. Pour over the port syrup and serve.

Nutritional information per portion: Energy 282kcal/1205kJ; Protein 3.7g; Carbohydrate 66.5g, of which sugars 66.5g; Fat 0.9g, of which saturates 0g; Cholesterol 0mg; Calcium 173mg; Fibre 5.4g; Sodium 50mg.

Baked bananas with ice cream

Baked bananas make the perfect partners for delicious vanilla ice cream topped with a toasted hazelnut sauce. This is a quick and easy dessert that looks as good as it tastes.

SERVES 4

4 large bananas
15ml/1 tbsp lemon juice
4 large scoops of Classic Vanilla ice cream

FOR THE SAUCE

25g/1oz/2 tbsp unsalted (sweet) butter
50g/2oz/¹⁄₂ cup hazelnuts, toasted and roughly chopped
45ml/3 tbsp golden (light corn) syrup
30ml/2 tbsp lemon juice

1 Preheat the oven to 180°C/350°F/Gas 4. Place the unpeeled bananas on a baking sheet and brush them with the lemon juice. Bake for about 20 minutes until the skins are turning black and the flesh gives a little when the bananas are gently squeezed.

2 Meanwhile, make the sauce. Melt the butter in a small pan. Add the hazelnuts and cook gently for 1 minute. Add the syrup and lemon juice and heat, stirring, for 1 minute more.

3 To serve, slit each banana open with a knife and open out the skins. Transfer to serving plates and serve with scoops of ice cream. Pour the sauce over.

COOK'S TIP
If you like, you can bake the bananas over the dying coals of a barbecue.
Put them on the rack as soon as you have removed all the main course items.

Nutritional information per portion: Energy 416kcal/1740kJ; Protein 6.3g; Carbohydrate 50.7g, of which sugars 47.2g; Fat 21.1g, of which saturates 9.5g; Cholesterol 35mg; Calcium 117mg; Fibre 1.9g; Sodium 124mg.

Baby Alaskas with liqueured apricots

Just as effective as a full-size baked Alaska, these delightful individual ices are concealed under their own little meringue mountains. You can also experiment with your favourite dried fruits.

SERVES 6

40g/1½oz/3 tbsp caster (superfine) sugar
60ml/4 tbsp water
150g/5oz/generous ½ cup ready-to-eat
    dried apricots, roughly chopped
30ml/2 tbsp Cointreau or other
    orange-flavoured liqueur

500ml/17fl oz/2¼ cups vanilla, honey or
    any nut-flavoured ice cream
6 large almond or ginger biscuits
3 egg whites
175g/6oz/scant 1 cup caster sugar

1 Heat the sugar and water in a small, heavy pan, stirring until the sugar dissolves. Add the apricots and simmer gently for 5 minutes until they have absorbed most of the syrup. Stir in the liqueur and leave to chill.

2 Freeze six small dariole moulds or metal dessert moulds for 15 minutes. Remove the ice cream from the freezer and leave for 15 minutes. With a dessertspoon, pack most of the ice cream into the moulds, leaving a deep cavity in the centre. Return each mould to the freezer once completed.

3 When all the moulds have been lined with ice cream, remove them from the freezer again and fill the centres with the apricots. Cover the apricots with more ice cream and freeze until firm.

4 Dip each mould in very hot water for 1–2 seconds, then invert. Slide a biscuit under each ice cream and transfer to a baking sheet. Place in the freezer.

5 Whisk the egg whites in a clean bowl until stiff. Gradually whisk in tablespoonfuls of caster sugar, whisking well each time until the mixture has become stiff and glossy.

6 With a palette knife, spread a thick layer of the meringue over each ice cream, making sure it meets the biscuits and seals in the ice cream. Swirl the surface decoratively. Return to the freezer.

7 About 15 minutes before serving, preheat the oven to 230°C/450°F/Gas 8. Bake the Alaskas for about 2 minutes until the meringue is pale golden. Serve immediately.

Nutritional information per portion: Energy 403kcal/1704kJ; Protein 6.2g; Carbohydrate 74.8g, of which sugars 68.6g; Fat 8.6g, of which saturates 5.9g; Cholesterol 26mg; Calcium 159mg; Fibre 1.7g; Sodium 127mg.

Coconut and passion fruit Alaska

Baked Alaska lends itself to many variations on a basic theme. This version comprises passion fruit, coconut sponge, tropical-fruit ice cream and delicious coconut-flavoured meringue.

SERVES 8

115g/4oz/1/2 cup unsalted (sweet)
   butter, softened
115g/4oz/generous 1/2 cup caster
   (superfine) sugar
2 eggs
115g/4oz/1 cup self-raising (self-rising) flour
2.5ml/1/2 tsp baking powder
5ml/1 tsp almond extract
40g/11/2oz/1/2 cup desiccated (dry,
   unsweetened shredded) coconut

15ml/1 tbsp milk
1 litre/13/4 pints/4 cups passion fruit
   ice cream
60ml/4 tbsp Kirsch
3 passion fruit
3 egg whites
115g/4oz/generous 1/2 cup caster sugar
50g/2oz/1/2 cup creamed coconut, grated

1 Preheat the oven to 180°C/350°F/Gas 4. Grease and line an 18cm/7in round cake tin (pan). Put all the sponge ingredients in a bowl and whisk until smooth. Spoon into the prepared tin, level the surface and bake for 35 minutes until the sponge is just firm. Leave to cool on a wire rack.

2 Dampen a 1.2 litre/2 pint/5 cup bowl and line it with clear film (plastic wrap). Remove the ice cream from the freezer for 15 minutes to soften slightly. Pack it into the lined bowl and return it to the freezer for 1 hour. Place the sponge on a small baking sheet or ovenproof plate and drizzle the surface with Kirsch. Remove the pulp from the fruit and scoop over the sponge.

3 Dip the bowl with the ice cream into very hot water for about 2 seconds to loosen the shaped ice cream. Invert it on to the sponge. Peel away the clear film and put the cake and ice cream in the freezer.

4 Whisk the egg whites in a clean bowl until stiff. Add a tablespoon of sugar at a time, whisking well each time, until the meringue is thick and glossy. Fold in the grated creamed coconut. With a metal spatula, spread the meringue all over the ice cream and sponge. Return to the freezer.

5 About 15 minutes before serving, preheat the oven to 220°C/425°F/Gas 7. Bake for 4–5 minutes, watching closely, until the peaks are golden. Serve immediately.

Nutritional information per portion: Energy 615kcal/2576kJ; Protein 9.5g; Carbohydrate 75.3g, of which sugars 63.1g; Fat 30.9g, of which saturates 20.8g; Cholesterol 111mg; Calcium 189mg; Fibre 1.4g; Sodium 212mg.

Toasted marzipan parcels with plums

Melting ice cream in lightly toasted marzipan makes an irresistible dessert for anyone who likes the flavour of almonds. You can use apricots, cherries or pears instead of plums, if you prefer.

SERVES 4

400g/14oz golden marzipan
icing (confectioners') sugar, for dusting
250ml/8fl oz/1 cup Classic Vanilla
 ice cream

FOR THE PLUM COMPOTE
3 red plums, about 250g/9oz
25g/1oz/2 tbsp caster (superfine) sugar
75ml/5 tbsp water

1 Roll out the marzipan on a surface lightly dusted with sifted icing sugar to a 45 x 23cm/18 x 9in rectangle. Then stamp out eight rounds using a plain 12cm/4^1/$_2$in biscuit cutter.

2 Place a spoonful of the ice cream in the centre of one of the circles. Bring the marzipan up over the ice cream and press the edges together to completely encase.

3 Crimp the edges with your fingers. Transfer to a small baking sheet and freeze. Fill and shape the remaining parcels in the same way and then freeze overnight.

4 Halve and stone (pit) the plums. Heat the sugar and water in a heavy pan, stirring until the sugar has completely dissolved.

5 Add the plums and cook very gently until tender but holding their shape. Test with the tip of a knife.

6 Preheat the grill (broiler) to high. Cook the marzipan parcels on the rack for 1–2 minutes, watching closely, until the crimped edge of the marzipan is lightly browned. Transfer the parcels to serving plates and serve with the warm plum compote.

Nutritional information per portion: Energy 547kcal/2307kJ; Protein 8g; Carbohydrate 92g, of which sugars 91.3g; Fat 18.1g, of which saturates 4.9g; Cholesterol 15mg; Calcium 140mg; Fibre 2.9g; Sodium 59mg.

Orange crêpes with mascarpone cream

With this delicious recipe, which is neither too rich nor too sweet, the sorbet and mascarpone simply melt together in their crisp, delicate pancake cases.

SERVES 8

FOR THE CRÊPES
115g/4oz/1 cup plain (all-purpose) flour
300ml/½ pint/1¼ cups milk
1 egg, plus 1 egg yolk
finely grated rind of 1 orange
30ml/2 tbsp caster (superfine) sugar
oil, for frying

TO FINISH
250g/9oz/generous 1 cup mascarpone
15ml/1 tbsp icing (confectioners') sugar
90ml/6 tbsp single (light) cream
45ml/3 tbsp Cointreau or orange juice
500ml/17fl oz/2¼ cups Orange Sorbet
icing sugar, for dusting

1 Blend the flour, milk, egg, egg yolk, orange rind and sugar in a food processor until smooth. Pour into a jug and leave for 30 minutes.

2 Heat a little oil in a medium frying pan or crêpe pan until very hot. Drain off the excess. Pour a little batter into the pan, tilting it so that the batter coats the base thinly. Pour any excess back into the jug.

3 Cook until the underside is golden, then flip and cook the other side. Slide on to a plate. Cook seven more, lightly oiling the pan each time.

4 Preheat the oven to 200°C/400°F/Gas 6. In a bowl, beat the mascarpone, the icing sugar, cream and liqueur or orange juice until smooth. Spread the mixture on the crêpes, taking it almost to the edges.

5 With a dessertspoon, scoop and arrange shavings of sorbet to one side of each topped crêpe. Fold the crêpes in half and dust with icing sugar. Fold again into quarters and dust again. Lay the crêpes in a large shallow baking dish and bake for 2 minutes until the sorbet starts to melt. Serve immediately.

Nutritional information per portion: Energy 316kcal/1324kJ; Protein 5.6g; Carbohydrate 34.2g, of which sugars 19.6g; Fat 17.2g, of which saturates 10.1g; Cholesterol 103mg; Calcium 100mg; Fibre 0.6g; Sodium 152mg.

Filo, ice cream and mincemeat parcels

These golden parcels reveal hot mincemeat and melting vanilla ice cream when cut open, and can be assembled days in advance.

MAKES 12

1 firm pear
225g/8oz/1 cup mincemeat
finely grated rind of 1 lemon
12 sheets of filo pastry, thawed if frozen
a little beaten egg
250ml/8 fl oz/1 cup Classic Vanilla ice cream
oil, for deep frying
caster (superfine) sugar for dusting

1 Peel, core and chop the pear, and stir in a small bowl with the mincemeat and lemon rind. Cut one filo sheet into two 20cm/8in squares. Brush one square lightly with beaten egg, then cover with the second square.

2 Lay 10ml/2 tsp mincemeat on the filo, placing it 2.5cm/1in away from one edge, spreading to cover a 7.5cm/3in area. Lay 10ml/2 tsp of the ice cream over the mincemeat. Brush around the edges with beaten egg.

3 Fold over the two opposite sides of the pastry to cover the filling. Roll up the strip, starting at the filled end. Transfer to a baking sheet and freeze. Make 11 more rolls.

4 Pour oil into a heavy pan to a depth of 7.5cm/3in. Heat it to 185°C/365°F. Fry several parcels at a time for 1–2 minutes until pale golden, turning during cooking. Drain on kitchen paper, dust with sugar and serve.

Nutritional information per portion: Energy 183kcal/764kJ; Protein 1.6g; Carbohydrate 23.3g, of which sugars 16.8g; Fat 9.9g, of which saturates 1.9g; Cholesterol 2mg; Calcium 35mg; Fibre 0.8g; Sodium 17mg.

Walnut and vanilla ice palmiers

These walnut pastries can be served freshly baked, but best make them ahead and reheat them in a moderate oven for 5 minutes.

MAKES 6

75g/3oz/³/₄ cup walnut pieces
350g/12oz puff pastry, thawed if frozen
beaten egg, to glaze
45ml/3 tbsp caster (superfine) sugar
about 200ml/7fl oz/scant 1 cup Classic Vanilla ice cream

1 Preheat the oven to 200°C/400°F/Gas 6. Lightly grease a large baking sheet with butter. Chop the walnuts finely. On a lightly floured surface, roll the pastry to a thin rectangle 30 x 20cm/12 x 8in.

2 Trim the edges of the pastry, then brush with the egg. Sprinkle all but 45ml/3 tbsp of the walnuts and 30ml/2 tbsp of the sugar. Run the rolling pin over the walnuts to press them into the pastry.

3 Roll up the pastry from one short side to the centre, then roll up the other side until the two rolls meet. Brush the points where the rolls meet with a little beaten egg. Cut the pastry into slices 1cm/¹/₂in thick.

4 Flatten the slices with a rolling pin. Transfer to the baking sheet. Brush with more of the beaten egg and sprinkle with the reserved walnuts and sugar.

5 Bake for about 15 minutes until pale golden. Serve warm, in pairs, sandwiched with ice cream.

Nutritional information per portion: Energy 398kcal/1661kJ; Protein 6.4g; Carbohydrate 38g, of which sugars 16.3g; Fat 25.7g, of which saturates 2.8g; Cholesterol 10mg; Calcium 93mg; Fibre 0.4g; Sodium 205mg.

Blueberry and vanilla crumble torte

In this heavenly pudding, vanilla ice cream is packed into a buttery crumble case and baked until the ice cream starts to melt over the crumble. It must be made the day before you intend to serve it.

SERVES 8

225g/8oz/2 cups plain (all-purpose) flour
5ml/1 tsp baking powder
175g/6oz/³/₄ cup unsalted (sweet)
    butter, diced
150g/5oz/³/₄ cup caster (superfine) sugar
1 egg
75g/3oz/³/₄ cup ground almonds

10ml/2 tsp natural vanilla extract
5ml/1 tsp mixed (apple pie) spice
500ml/17fl oz/2¹/₄ cups Classic Vanilla
    ice cream
175g/6oz/1¹/₂ cups blueberries
icing (confectioners') sugar, for dusting

1 Preheat the oven to 180°C/350°F/Gas 4. Put the flour and baking powder in a food processor. Add the butter and process briefly to mix. Add the sugar and process briefly again until the mixture is crumbly. Remove about 175g/6oz/1¹/₂ cups of the crumble mixture and set this aside.

2 Add the egg, ground almonds, vanilla extract and mixed spice to the remaining crumble mixture and blend to a paste.

3 Scrape the paste into a 20cm/8in springform tin (pan). Press it firmly on to the base and halfway up the sides to make an even case. Line the pastry case with baking parchment and fill with baking beans.

4 Sprinkle the reserved crumble mixture on to a baking sheet and place in the oven with the pastry case. Bake the crumble for 20 minutes and the case for about 30 minutes until pale golden. Remove the paper and beans from the case and bake it for 5 minutes more. Leave both the crumble and the case to cool.

5 Pack the ice cream into the almond pastry case and level the surface. Then scatter with the blueberries followed by the baked crumble mixture. Freeze overnight.

6 About 25 minutes before serving, preheat the oven to 180°C/350°F/Gas 4. Bake the torte for 10–15 minutes, until the ice cream has started to soften. Dust with icing sugar and serve in wedges.

Nutritional information per portion: Energy 522kcal/2183kJ; Protein 8.1g; Carbohydrate 57.7g, of which sugars 34.4g; Fat 29.7g, of which saturates 15.9g; Cholesterol 86mg; Calcium 142mg; Fibre 2g; Sodium 182mg.

Hot ice cream fritters

Deep-fried ice cream may seem odd, but once you've made these crisp fritters, you'll be converted. The secret is to encase the ice cream thoroughly in two layers of sweet biscuit crumb. This turns crisp and golden during frying, leaving the ice cream to melt only slightly.

SERVES 4

750ml/1¼ pints/3 cups firm Vanilla ice cream

115g/4oz amaretti or ratafia biscuits (almond macaroons)

115g/4oz/2 cups fresh brown breadcrumbs

1 egg

45g/1¾oz/3 tbsp plain (all-purpose) flour

oil, for deep frying

FOR THE CARAMEL SAUCE

115g/4oz/generous ½ cup caster (superfine) sugar

150ml/¼ pint/²⁄₃ cup water

150ml|/¼ pint/²⁄₃ cup double (heavy) cream

1 Line a baking sheet with baking parchment and put it in the freezer for 15 minutes, at the same time removing the ice cream from the freezer to soften slightly. Scoop about 12 balls of ice cream, making them as round as possible and place them on the lined baking sheet. Freeze for at least 1 hour until firm.

2 Meanwhile, put the amaretti or ratafia biscuits in a strong plastic bag and crush them with a rolling pin. Tip into a bowl and add the breadcrumbs. Mix well, and then transfer half the mixture to a plate. Beat the egg in a shallow dish. Sprinkle the flour on to a second plate.

3 Using cool hands, and working very quickly, roll each ice cream ball in the flour, then dip in the beaten egg until coated. Roll the balls in the mixed crumbs until completely covered. Return the coated ice cream balls to the baking sheet and freeze for at least 1 hour more.

4 Repeat the process, using the remaining flour, egg and breadcrumbs, so that each ball has an additional coating. Return the ice cream balls to the freezer for at least 4 hours, preferably overnight.

5 Make the sauce. Heat the sugar and water in a small, heavy pan, stirring occasionally, until the sugar has dissolved. Bring to the boil and boil the syrup for about 10 minutes without stirring until deep golden. Immediately immerse the base of the pan in a bowl of cold water to prevent the syrup from cooking any more.

6 Pour the cream into the syrup and return the pan to the heat. Stir until the sauce is smooth. Set aside while you fry the ice cream.

7 Pour oil into a heavy pan to a depth of 7.5cm/3in. Heat to 185°C/365°F or until a cube of bread added to the oil browns in 30 seconds. Add several of the ice cream balls and fry for about 1 minute until the coating on each is golden. Drain on kitchen paper and quickly cook the remainder in the same way. Serve the fritters with the caramel sauce.

Nutritional information per portion: Energy 1064kcal/4453kJ; Protein 15.1g; Carbohydrate 121.6g, of which sugars 77g; Fat 58.6g, of which saturates 28.1g; Cholesterol 145mg; Calcium 319mg; Fibre 1.4g; Sodium 454mg.

Syrupy brioche slices with vanilla ice cream

Keep a few individual brioche buns in the freezer to make this fabulous five-minute pudding. For a slightly tarter taste, use lemon instead of orange rind.

SERVES 4

butter, for greasing
finely grated rind and juice of 1 orange
50g/2oz/$\frac{1}{4}$ cup caster (superfine) sugar
90ml/6 tbsp water
1.5ml/$\frac{1}{4}$ tsp ground cinnamon

4 brioche buns
15ml/1 tbsp icing (confectioners') sugar
400ml/14fl oz/1$\frac{2}{3}$ cups Classic Vanilla
   ice cream

1 Lightly grease a gratin dish and set aside. Put the orange rind and juice, sugar, water and cinnamon in a heavy pan. Heat gently, stirring, until the sugar has dissolved, then boil for 2 minutes without stirring.

2 Remove the syrup from the heat and pour it into a shallow heatproof dish. Preheat the grill (broiler). Cut each brioche vertically into three thick slices. Dip one side of each slice in the hot syrup and arrange in the gratin dish, syrupy sides down. Reserve the remaining syrup. Grill (broil) the brioche until lightly toasted.

3 Turn over and dust with icing sugar. Grill for 2–3 minutes more until they begin to caramelize around the edges.

4 Transfer to serving plates and top with scoops of ice cream. Spoon over the remaining syrup and serve immediately.

Nutritional information per portion: Energy 399kcal/1681kJ; Protein 8.5g; Carbohydrate 65.5g, of which sugars 42.5g; Fat 12g, of which saturates 7.2g; Cholesterol 25mg; Calcium 174mg; Fibre 1.3g; Sodium 252mg.

Peach, blackberry and ice cream gratin

A wonderfully easy dessert in which the flavours of large ripe peaches, blackberries, ice cream and brown sugar mingle together as they grill.

SERVES 4

4 large peaches
15ml/1 tbsp lemon juice
**120ml/4fl oz/½ cup Classic Vanilla
    ice cream**
115g/4oz/1 cup small blackberries
**40g/1½ oz/3 tbsp light muscovado
    (brown) sugar**

1 Preheat the grill (broiler). Cut the peaches in half and remove the stones (pits). Cut a thin slice off the rounded side of each peach so that they sit flat on the surface.

2 Brush the cut surfaces with lemon juice and transfer to a shallow flameproof dish. Grill (broil) for 2 minutes. Remove from the heat, but leave the grill on in order to maintain the same temperature.

3 Pack small teaspoon-sized scoops of the ice cream into the peach halves, piling them up in the centre. Add the blackberries, pushing them gently into the ice cream.

4 Sprinkle the filled peaches with the muscovado sugar and replace under the hot grill for 1–2 minutes until the sugar has dissolved and the ice cream is beginning to melt. Serve immediately.

Nutritional information per portion: Energy 138kcal/583kJ; Protein 2.4g; Carbohydrate 26.8g, of which sugars 26.4g; Fat 2.7g, of which saturates 1.8g; Cholesterol 7mg; Calcium 55mg; Fibre 2.4g; Sodium 20mg.

Apple ice cream with cinnamon bread

Cooking the apples with butter, lemon and spice accentuates their flavour and makes an ice cream that is excellent with apple pies, other pastries and fried sugared bread.

SERVES 6

675g/1¹/₂lb cooking apples, peeled, cored and sliced

1.5ml/¹/₄ tsp mixed (apple pie) spice

finely grated rind and juice of 1 lemon

50g/2oz/¹/₄ cup unsalted (sweet) butter

90g/3¹/₂oz/scant ¹/₂ cup cream cheese

2 egg whites, beaten

150ml/¹/₄ pint/²/₃ cup double (heavy) cream

mint sprigs, to decorate

FOR THE CINNAMON BREAD

6 thick slices of white bread

1 egg, beaten

1 egg yolk

2.5ml/¹/₂ tsp natural vanilla extract

150ml/¹/₄ pint/²/₃ cup single (light) cream

65g/2¹/₂oz/5 tbsp caster (superfine) sugar

2.5ml/¹/₂ tsp ground cinnamon

25g/1oz/2 tbsp unsalted (sweet) butter

45ml/3 tbsp oil

1 Gently cook the apples, spice and lemon rind in butter in a covered pan for 10 minutes. Leave to cool.

2 Blend the apples and juices, lemon juice and cream cheese in a food processor until smooth. In separate bowls, whisk the egg whites until stiff, and the cream to form soft peaks.

3 Scrape the purée into a bowl. Fold in the cream, then the egg whites. Freeze overnight in a plastic tub.

4 Make the cinnamon bread 20 minutes before serving. Cut the crusts off each bread slice, then cut diagonally in half. Beat together the egg, egg yolk, vanilla extract, cream and 15ml/1 tbsp of the sugar.

5 Arrange the bread triangles in a single layer on a large, shallow plate or tray. Pour over the cream mixture and leave for 10 minutes.

6 Mix the remaining sugar with the cinnamon on a plate. Melt the butter in the oil in a frying pan. When hot, add half the bread and fry until golden underneath. Turn with a metal spatula and fry the other side.

7 Drain the slices on kitchen paper, then coat both sides in cinnamon sugar, keeping them hot. Cook the remaining slices in the same way. Serve at once, topped with scoops of the apple ice cream. Decorate with the mint sprigs.

Nutritional information per portion: Energy 535kcal/2227kJ; Protein 5.7g; Carbohydrate 34.7g, of which sugars 23g; Fat 42.6g, of which saturates 23.3g; Cholesterol 123mg; Calcium 94mg; Fibre 2.2g; Sodium 288mg.

Herb, spice & flower ices

For those with more adventurous tastes, this chapter features an intriguing repertoire of less predictable flavours such as Turkish delight, lavender, saffron and even chilli. The ices in the following collection are quick and easy to make, and will have everyone guessing the ingredients.

Rosemary ice cream

Fresh rosemary works as well in sweet dishes as it does in savoury. Serve this ice cream as an accompaniment to soft fruit or plum compote, or on its own, with amaretti.

SERVES 6

300ml/½ pint/1¼ cups milk
4 large fresh rosemary sprigs
3 egg yolks
75g/3oz/6 tbsp caster (superfine) sugar
10ml/2 tsp cornflour (cornstarch)
400ml/14fl oz/1⅔ cups crème fraîche
about 15ml/1 tbsp demerara (raw) sugar
fresh rosemary sprigs and herb flowers,
    to decorate
amaretti or ratafia biscuits (almond
    macaroons), to serve

1 Put the milk and rosemary sprigs in a heavy pan. Bring almost to the boil, remove from the heat and leave to infuse for about 20 minutes. Place the egg yolks in a bowl and whisk in the sugar and the cornflour.

2 Return the pan to the heat and bring almost to the boil. Gradually pour over the yolk mixture and stir it in well. Return to the pan and cook over a very gentle heat, stirring constantly until it thickens. Do not let it boil or it may curdle.

3 Strain the custard into a bowl. Cover closely with baking parchment, leave to cool, then chill until very cold. Stir in the crème fraîche.

4 Pour into a container and freeze for 3–4 hours, beating twice. Return to the freezer until ready to serve.

5 Transfer to the fridge 30 minutes before serving. Scoop into dessert dishes, sprinkle with demerara sugar and decorate with fresh rosemary sprigs and herb flowers. Serve with ratafia biscuits.

Nutritional information per portion: Energy 371kcal/1538kJ; Protein 4.7g; Carbohydrate 21.2g, of which sugars 19.4g; Fat 30.3g, of which saturates 19.4g; Cholesterol 179mg; Calcium 119mg; Fibre 0g; Sodium 43mg.

Lavender and honey ice cream

In this elegant ice cream, lavender and honey make a memorable partnership. Serve scooped into glasses or set in little moulds, topped with whipped cream and decorated with lavender flowers.

SERVES 6–8

90ml/6 tbsp clear honey

4 egg yolks

10ml/2 tsp cornflour (cornstarch)

8 lavender sprigs, plus extra, to decorate

450ml/³⁄₄ pint/scant 2 cups milk

450ml/³⁄₄ pint/scant 2 cups whipping cream

dessert biscuits, to serve

1 Put the honey, egg yolk, and cornflour in a bowl. Separate the lavender flowers and add them plus a little milk. Whisk lightly. In a heavy pan bring the remaining milk to the boil. Add to the egg yolk mixture, stirring well.

2 Return the mixture to the pan and cook very gently, stirring until the mixture has thickened. Then pour into a bowl.

3 Cover the surface closely with a circle of baking parchment and leave to cool, then chill until very cold.

4 Whip the cream and fold into the custard. Pour into a tub and freeze for 3–4 hours, beating twice.

5 Transfer to the fridge 30 minutes before serving, with dessert biscuits, in small dishes, decorated with lavender flowers.

Nutritional information per portion: Energy 308kcal/1275kJ; Protein 4.5g; Carbohydrate 13.9g, of which sugars 12.8g; Fat 26.4g, of which saturates 15.6g; Cholesterol 163mg; Calcium 113mg; Fibre 0g; Sodium 45mg.

Star anise and grapefruit granita

With its aniseed flavour and dramatic appearance, star anise makes an interesting and decorative addition to many fruit desserts.

SERVES 6

200g/7oz/1 cup caster (superfine) sugar
450ml/³⁄₄ pint/scant 2 cups water
6 whole star anise
4 grapefruit

1 Gently heat the sugar and water in a pan, stirring occasionally, until the sugar has completely dissolved. Stir in the star anise and heat gently for 2 minutes, without stirring. Remove from the heat and leave to cool.

2 Take a slice off the top and bottom of each grapefruit, then slice off the skin and pith. Chop the flesh roughly and blend in a food processor until almost smooth. Press the pulp through a sieve (strainer) into a bowl.

3 Strain the syrup into the bowl, reserving the star anise. Mix well, then cover and freeze the mixture in a shallow freezerproof container for about 2 hours until ice crystals form around the edges of the container.

4 Using a fork, break up the ice crystals, then return the mixture to the freezer. Freeze for 30 minutes more, mash with a fork again, then return to the freezer. Repeat the process until the mixture forms fine ice crystals.

5 To serve, spoon the granita into glasses and decorate with the reserved star anise.

Nutritional information per portion: Energy 166kcal/707kJ; Protein 1.1g; Carbohydrate 42.8g, of which sugars 42.8g; Fat 0.1g, of which saturates 0g; Cholesterol 0mg; Calcium 45mg; Fibre 1.5g; Sodium 6mg.

Basil and orange granita

More often associated with savoury dishes, basil has a sweet, aromatic flavour that complements tangy oranges beautifully.

SERVES 6

5 large oranges
175g/6oz/scant 1 cup caster (superfine) sugar
450ml/³⁄₄ pint/scant 2 cups water
orange juice (if necessary)
15g/¹⁄₂oz/¹⁄₂ cup fresh basil leaves
tiny fresh basil leaves, to decorate

1 Gently heat the thinly pared rinds of three oranges, the sugar and water in a pan until the sugar has dissolved. Cool, pour into a bowl and chill.

2 Put the juice from all the oranges into a large measuring jug (500ml/17fl oz/2¹⁄₄ cups). Top up with fresh orange juice if necessary. In short bursts, blend the juice and basil leaves in a food processor or blender until the basil has been chopped into small pieces.

3 Using a slotted spoon, remove the orange rind from the chilled syrup. Stir in the orange juice and basil mixture, then cover and freeze in a freezerproof container for about 2 hours or until it is mushy around the edges. Break the ice crystals with a fork and stir well. Freeze for 30 more minutes, mash with a fork and return to the freezer. Repeat until the ice forms fine crystals.

4 Spoon the granita into tall glasses and decorate with the tiny basil leaves.

Nutritional information per portion: Energy 189kcal/806kJ; Protein 2.4g; Carbohydrate 47.5g, of which sugars 47.5g; Fat 0.2g, of which saturates 0g; Cholesterol 0mg; Calcium 110mg; Fibre 3.4g; Sodium 12mg.

Bay and ratafia slice

The warm but delicate flavour of bay leaves works surprisingly well with ices and combines very effectively with almond flavours. Serve with fresh apricots, plums, peaches or soft fruits.

SERVES 6

300ml/½ pint/1¼ cups milk
4 fresh bay leaves
4 egg yolks
75g/3oz/6 tbsp caster (superfine) sugar
10ml/2 tsp cornflour (cornstarch)
150g/5oz ratafia biscuits
    (almond macaroons)
300ml/½ pint/1¼ cups whipping cream

1 Bring the milk and bay leaves to the boil in a pan. Remove from the heat and leave infusing for 30 minutes. Whisk the egg yolks in a bowl with the sugar and cornflour.

2 Strain the milk over the egg yolk mixture and stir well. Return to the pan and gently heat, stirring constantly until the custard thickens. Do not let it boil. Transfer the custard to a bowl, cover the surface closely with baking parchment and leave to cool completely. Chill until very cold.

3 Place the biscuits in a plastic bag and crush them using a rolling pin. In a separate bowl lightly whip the cream and fold into the chilled custard, then stir in 50g/2oz of the crushed biscuits.

4 Working quickly, spoon the ice cream on to a sheet of baking parchment, packing it into a log shape, about 6cm/2½in thick and 25cm/10in long.

5 Bring the greaseproof up around the ice cream to pack it together tightly and give it a good shape. Support the ice cream log on a baking sheet and freeze for at least 3 hours or overnight.

6 Spread the remaining crushed biscuits on a sheet of baking parchment. Unwrap the ice cream log and roll it quickly in the crumbs to coat. Return to the freezer until needed. Serve in slices.

Nutritional information per portion: Energy 451kcal/ 1881kJ; Protein 7.7g; Carbohydrate 38.1g, of which sugars 25.7g; Fat 30.9g, of which saturates 16.5g; Cholesterol 298mg; Calcium 157mg; Fibre 0.4g; Sodium 129mg.

Saffron, apricot and almond cream

This vibrant ice cream has a slightly Middle-Eastern flavour. Although expensive, saffron's intense colour and distinctive flavour are well worth it, and you only need a small amount.

SERVES 6–8

150g/5oz/²/₃ cup dried apricots

60ml/4 tbsp Cointreau or other orange-flavoured liqueur

2.5ml/¹/₂ tsp saffron strands, lightly crushed

15ml/1 tbsp boiling water

3 egg yolks

75g/3oz/6 tbsp caster (superfine) sugar

10ml/2 tsp cornflour (cornstarch)

300ml/¹/₂ pint/1¹/₄ cups milk

300ml/¹/₂ pint/1¹/₄ cups single (light) cream

75g/3oz/³/₄ cup unblanched almonds, lightly toasted

amaretti, to serve (optional)

1 Put small pieces of chopped apricots into a bowl. Add the liqueur and leave for about 1 hour or until absorbed. Put the saffron in a cup with the boiling water and leave to stand while you make the custard.

2 Whisk the egg yolks, sugar, cornflour and a little milk in a bowl. Pour the milk into a pan, bring it almost to the boil, then pour it over the yolk mixture, stirring. Return to the pan and cook very gently, stirring until it thickens. Do not let it boil.

3 Stir in the saffron, with its liquid, then cover the surface of the custard with baking parchment and leave it to cool. Chill until it is very cold.

4 Whip the cream and fold into the custard. Add the apricots and nuts and pour the mixture into a container. Freeze for 3–4 hours, beating twice as it thickens and return to the freezer.

5 Transfer to the fridge 30 minutes before serving. Scoop into glasses and serve with amaretti. This dish looks particularly attractive served in small glasses or glass cups, if you have them.

Nutritional information per portion: Energy 240kcal/1003kJ; Protein 5.1g; Carbohydrate 19.3g, of which sugars 17.9g; Fat 14.6g, of which saturates 5.6g; Cholesterol 96mg; Calcium 84mg; Fibre 1.9g; Sodium 19mg.

Peppermint swirl

This ice cream looks most sophisticated, with its delicate colours and marbled appearance. The refreshing taste of peppermint makes it ideal for serving after a rich main course.

SERVES 6

75g/3oz/6 tbsp caster (superfine) sugar
60ml/4 tbsp water
10 large fresh peppermint sprigs
2.5ml/½ tsp peppermint essence
    (extract)
450ml/³/₄ pint/scant 2 cups double
    (heavy) cream
a few drops of green food colouring
200g/7oz/scant 1 cup Greek (strained
    plain) yogurt

1 Put the sugar, water and fresh peppermint in a small, heavy pan and heat gently, stirring occasionally, until the sugar has dissolved. Bring to the boil and cook without stirring for about 3 minutes to make a syrup.

2 Strain the syrup into a medium bowl and stir in the peppermint essence. Transfer 60ml/4 tbsp of the mixture to a large bowl.

3 Remove from the heat and leave to cool. Dampen a 450g/1lb loaf tin (pan) with a little water, then line it with clear film (plastic wrap).

4 Add 45ml/3 tbsp of the cream and a few drops of food colouring to the medium bowl and stir until smooth. Add the remaining cream to the mixture in the large bowl, then stir in the Greek yogurt. Whisk the mixture until it starts to hold its shape.

5 Place alternate spoonfuls of the two mixtures in the prepared tin. When the tin is full, swirl the two mixtures together, using a teaspoon. Cover and freeze for at least 4 hours or overnight.

6 To serve, dip the tin in very hot water for 1–2 seconds, then invert the frozen swirl on to a serving plate. Serve in slices.

Nutritional information per portion: Energy 460kcal/ 1900kJ; Protein 3.4g; Carbohydrate 15g, of which sugars 15g; Fat 43.7g, of which saturates 26.8g; Cholesterol 103mg; Calcium 93mg; Fibre 0g; Sodium 41mg.

Lemon and cardamom ice cream

The classic partnership of lemon and cardamom gives this rich ice cream a lovely "clean" tang. It is the perfect choice for serving after spicy dishes.

SERVES 6

15ml/1 tbsp cardamom pods
4 egg yolks
115g/4oz caster (superfine) sugar
10ml/2 tsp cornflour (cornstarch)
grated rind and juice of 3 lemons
300ml/¹/₂ pint/1¹/₄ cups milk
300ml/¹/₂ pint/1¹/₄ cups whipping cream
fresh lemon balm sprigs and icing
   (confectioners') sugar, to decorate

1 Put the cardamom pods in a mortar and crush them with a pestle to release the seeds. Pick out and discard the shells, then grind the seeds to break them up slightly.

2 Put the egg yolks, sugar, cornflour, lemon rind and juice in a bowl. Add the cardamom seeds and whisk well.

3 Bring the milk to the boil in a heavy pan, then pour it over the egg yolk mixture, stirring well. Return the mixture to the pan and cook over a very gentle heat, stirring constantly until the custard has thickened.

4 Pour the custard into a bowl, cover the surface closely with a circle of baking parchment and leave to cool. Chill until very cold.

5 Whip the cream lightly and fold into the custard. Pour into a container and freeze for 3–4 hours, beating twice as it thickens. Return to the freezer until required.

6 Transfer the ice cream to the fridge 30 minutes before serving to soften slightly. Scoop into glasses and decorate with the lemon balm and icing sugar.

Nutritional information per portion: Energy 338kcal/1406kJ; Protein 4.9g; Carbohydrate 25.3g, of which sugars 23.7g; Fat 24.9g, of which saturates 14.3g; Cholesterol 197mg; Calcium 116mg; Fibre 0g; Sodium 42mg.

Chilli sorbet

Served during or after dinner, this unusual but refreshing sorbet is sure to become a talking point among your guests. Use a medium-hot chilli rather than any of the fiery varieties.

SERVES 6

1 fresh red chilli
finely grated rind and juice of 2 lemons
finely grated rind and juice of 2 limes
225g/8oz/1 cup caster (superfine) sugar
750ml/1¼ pints/3 cups water
pared lemon or lime rind, to decorate

1 Cut the chilli in half, removing all the seeds and any pith with a small sharp knife, and then chop the flesh very finely.

2 Gently heat the chilli, lemon and lime rind, sugar and water in a heavy pan, stirring while the sugar dissolves. Bring to the boil and simmer for 2 minutes without stirring. Let cool.

3 Add lemon and lime juice to the chilli syrup and chill until very cold.

4 Pour into a container and freeze for 3–4 hours, beating twice. Return to the freezer until ready to serve.

5 Spoon into glasses and decorate with the thinly pared lemon or lime rind.

COOK'S TIP
For an added kick, drizzle with tequila or vodka before serving.

Nutritional information per portion: Energy 150kcal/640kJ; Protein 0.5g; Carbohydrate 39.4g, of which sugars 39.4g; Fat 0.1g, of which saturates 0g; Cholesterol 0mg; Calcium 23mg; Fibre 0g; Sodium 3mg.

Mulled wine sorbet

This dramatic-looking, spicy and flavoursome sorbet provides a brief and welcome respite from the general overindulgence that takes place during the festive season, or any other celebration.

SERVES 6

1 bottle medium red wine
2 clementines or 1 large orange
16 whole cloves
2 cinnamon sticks, halved
1 apple, roughly chopped
5ml/1 tsp mixed (apple pie) spice
75g/3oz/scant ¹/₂ cup light muscovado (brown) sugar
150ml/¹/₄ pint/²/₃ cup water
200ml/7fl oz/scant 1 cup freshly squeezed orange juice
45ml/3 tbsp brandy
strips of pared orange rind, to decorate

1 Gently heat the wine, clementines or oranges (halved and studded with cloves), cinnamon sticks, apple, mixed spice, sugar and water until the sugar dissolves. Cover the pan and cook the mixture gently for 15 minutes. Remove from the heat and leave to cool.

2 Strain the mixture into a large bowl, then stir in the orange juice and brandy. Chill until very cold.

3 Pour the mixture into a container and freeze for 3–4 hours, beating twice as it thickens. Return to the freezer until ready to serve.

4 To serve, spoon or scoop the sorbet into small glasses and decorate with the strips of pared orange rind.

Nutritional information per portion: Energy 163kcal/684kJ; Protein 0.4g; Carbohydrate 16.3g, of which sugars 16.3g; Fat 0g, of which saturates 0g; Cholesterol 0mg; Calcium 19mg; Fibre 0g; Sodium 13mg.

Turkish delight sorbet

Anyone who likes Turkish delight will adore this intriguing dessert. Because of its sweetness, it is best served in small portions and is simply delicious with after-dinner coffee.

SERVES 8

250g/9oz rose-water-flavoured
   Turkish delight
25g/1oz/2 tbsp caster (superfine) sugar
750ml/1¼ pints/3 cups water

30ml/2 tbsp lemon juice
50g/2oz white chocolate, broken into pieces
roughly chopped sugared almonds,
   to decorate

1 Cut the cubes of Turkish delight into small pieces. Put half the pieces in a heavy pan with the sugar. Pour in half the water. Heat gently until the Turkish delight has dissolved.

2 Cool, then stir in the lemon juice with the remaining water and Turkish delight. Chill well.

3 Pour the mixture into a container and freeze for 3–4 hours, beating twice with a fork as it thickens. Return it to the freezer until it is ready to serve. While the sorbet is freezing, dampen eight very small plastic cups or glasses, then line them with clear film (plastic wrap).

4 Spoon the sorbet into the cups and tap them lightly on the surface to compact the mixture. Cover with the overlapping film and freeze for at least 3 hours or overnight.

5 Make a paper piping bag. Put the chocolate in a heatproof bowl and melt it over a pan of gently simmering water.

6 Meanwhile, remove the sorbets from the freezer, let them stand at room temperature for 5 minutes, then pull them out of the cups. Transfer to serving plates and peel away the film. Spoon the melted chocolate into the piping bag, snip off the tip and scribble a design on the sorbet and the plate. Scatter the sugared almonds over and serve.

Nutritional information per portion: Energy 280kcal/1188kJ; Protein 1.4g; Carbohydrate 63.8g, of which sugars 58g; Fat 3.9g, of which saturates 2.3g; Cholesterol 0mg; Calcium 44mg; Fibre 0g; Sodium 34mg.

Rose geranium marquise

Rose geranium leaves give this ice cream a delicate, scented flavour. If you can't find savoiardi biscuits, ordinary sponge finger biscuits can be used instead.

SERVES 8

225g/8oz/generous 1 cup caster (superfine) sugar

400ml/14fl oz/1²/₃ cups water

24 fresh rose geranium leaves

45ml/3 tbsp lemon juice

250g/9oz/generous 1 cup mascarpone

300ml/¹/₂ pint/1¹/₄ cups double (heavy) or whipping cream

200g/7oz savoiardi or sponge finger biscuits

90g/3¹/₂oz/scant 1 cup almonds, finely chopped and toasted

geranium flowers and icing (confectioners') sugar, to decorate

1 Gently heat the sugar and water in a heavy pan, stirring until the sugar dissolves. Add the geranium leaves and cook gently for 2 minutes. Cool.

2 Strain the geranium syrup into a measuring jug and add the lemon juice. Beat the mascarpone in a bowl until softened. Gradually beat in 150ml/¹/₄ pint/²/₃ cup of the syrup mixture. Whip the cream until it forms peaks, then fold it into the mascarpone mixture. If the mixture doesn't hold its shape, whip a little more.

3 Spoon a little of the mixture on to a flat, freezerproof serving plate and spread it out to form a 21 x 12cm/8¹/₂ x 4¹/₂in rectangle. Pour the remaining syrup into a shallow bowl. Dip one third of the biscuits in the syrup until very moist but not actually disintegrating and arrange over the rectangle.

4 Spread another thin layer of the cream mixture over the biscuits. Set aside 15ml/1 tbsp of the nuts for the topping. Scatter half the remainder over the cream. Make a further two layers of syrup-steeped biscuits, sandwiching them with more cream and the remaining nuts, but leaving enough cream mixture to coat the dessert completely.

5 Spread the remaining cream mixture over the top and sides of the cake until it is evenly coated. Sprinkle with the reserved nuts. Freeze the marquise for at least 4 hours or overnight.

6 Transfer the marquise to the fridge for 30 minutes before serving, so that it softens slightly. Scatter with geranium flowers, dust with icing sugar, and serve in slices.

Nutritional information per portion: Energy 454kcal/1896kJ; Protein 8.6g; Carbohydrate 45.4g, of which sugars 39.6g; Fat 27.7g, of which saturates 13.3g; Cholesterol 109mg; Calcium 83mg; Fibre 1.1g; Sodium 34mg.

Elderflower and lime yogurt ice

These fragrant flowerheads are only in season for a short time. Fortunately, high-quality bought or home-made elderflower cordial combines well with limes to make a refreshing iced dessert.

SERVES 6

4 egg yolks
50g/2oz/1/4 cup caster (superfine) sugar
10ml/2 tsp cornflour (cornstarch)
300ml/1/2 pint/1 1/4 cups milk
finely grated rind and juice of 2 limes
150ml/1/4 pint/2/3 cup
   elderflower cordial
200ml/7fl oz/scant 1 cup Greek (strained
   plain) yogurt
150ml/1/4 pint/2/3 cup double
   (heavy) cream
grated lime, to decorate

1 Whisk the egg yolks in a bowl with the sugar, cornflour and a little of the milk. Bring the remaining milk to the boil in a heavy pan, then pour it over the yolk mixture, whisking constantly. Return to the pan and cook gently, stirring until the custard thickens. Do not let it boil.

2 Pour the custard into a bowl. Add the lime rind and juice and pour in the elderflower cordial. Mix lightly. Cover the surface of the mixture closely with baking parchment. Leave to cool, then chill.

3 Whip the yogurt and cream and fold into the custard. Pour the mixture into a freezerproof container and freeze for 3–4 hours, beating twice with a fork or electric mixer as it thickens.

4 Scoop into individual dishes and return to the freezer until ready to serve.

5 Transfer the yogurt ice to the fridge 30 minutes before serving. Decorate with the grated lime rind and serve.

Nutritional information per portion: Energy 219kcal/912kJ; Protein 4.3g; Carbohydrate 12.4g, of which sugars 10.9g; Fat 17.7g, of which saturates 10.6g; Cholesterol 37mg; Calcium 125mg; Fibre 0g; Sodium 54mg.

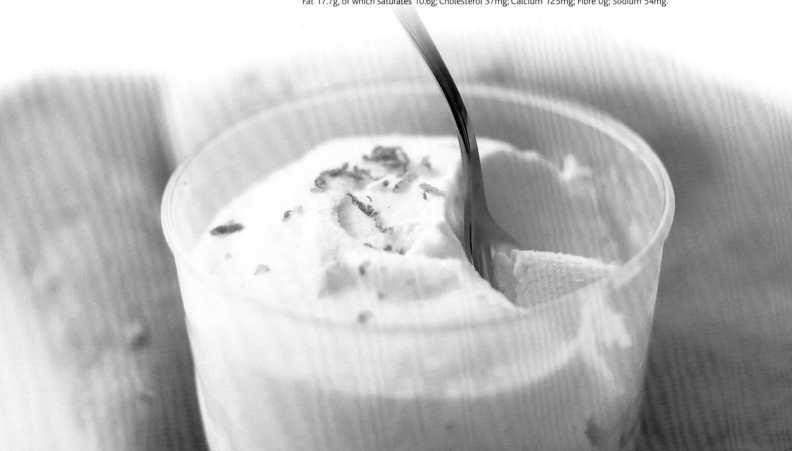

Pomegranate and orange flower water creams

The colour of this dessert will range from pastel pink to vibrant cerise, depending on the type of pomegranate used, but whatever the shade, the finished result will be very impressive.

SERVES 6

10ml/2 tsp cornflour (cornstarch)
300ml/¹⁄₂ pint/1¹⁄₄ cups milk
25g/1oz/2 tbsp caster (superfine) sugar
2 large pomegranates
30ml/2 tbsp orange flower water
75ml/5 tbsp grenadine
300ml/¹⁄₂ pint/1¹⁄₄ cups whipping cream
extra pomegranate seeds and orange
**   flower water, to serve**

1 Put the cornflour into a pan and blend to a paste with a little milk. Stir in the remaining milk and the sugar and cook, stirring until thickened. Pour it into a bowl, cover with baking parchment and leave to cool.

2 Halve the pomegranates, squeeze out the juice, with a lemon squeezer, and add it to the cornflour mixture, with the orange flower water, grenadine and cream.

3 Stir to mix, then pour into a container and freeze for 3–4 hours, beating twice as it thickens.

4 Spoon the ice cream into one large, or six individual, freezerproof serving dishes and freeze for 2 hours, or overnight.

5 Transfer to the fridge 30 minutes before serving to soften. Top with pomegranate seeds tossed in the extra orange flower water.

Nutritional information per portion: Energy 278kcal/1151kJ; Protein 2.8g; Carbohydrate 10.6g, of which sugars 9.1g; Fat 22.1g, of which saturates 13.9g; Cholesterol 60mg; Calcium 101mg; Fibre 0.6g; Sodium 36mg.

Iced drinks

Keep a supply of classic ice creams

and sorbets for making a whole range

of exciting drinks. Blend with a splash

of liqueur for a cooler drink with a kick,

scoop into glasses and top up with fizz,

or mix with fruit for a wonderful drink

and dessert in one.

Iced Margaritas

This smooth, cooling sorbet drink has all the punch of Mexico's renowned cocktail. Serve it in tall, slim glasses, decorated with slices of lemon and lime.

SERVES 2

35ml/7 tsp freshly squeezed lime juice
a little caster (superfine) sugar, for frosting
4 lime and 4 lemon slices
60ml/4 tbsp tequila
30ml/2 tbsp Cointreau
6–8 small scoops of Orange or Lime Sorbet
150ml/$^1/_4$ pint/$^2/_3$ cup chilled lemonade
sprigs of lemon balm, to decorate

1 Brush the rims of two tall glasses with 5ml/1 tsp of the lime juice. Spread out the sugar on a plate. Dip the rims of the glasses in the sugar to give a frosted edge.

2 Carefully add two lime and two lemon slices, stood on end, to each glass.

3 Mix the tequila, Cointreau and remaining lime juice in a bowl. Scoop the sorbet into the glasses.

4 Spoon an equal quantity of the tequila mixture into each glass. Top up with the lemonade and serve immediately, decorated with lemon balm.

VARIATION
For a "shorter" version of this drink, use cocktail glasses and just one scoop of sorbet. The rims of the glasses can be frosted with salt instead of sugar, as for traditional Margaritas.

Nutritional information per portion: Energy 368kcal/1524kJ; Protein 0.1g; Carbohydrate 0.3g, of which sugars 0.3g; Fat 0g, of which saturates 0g; Cholesterol 0mg; Calcium 2mg; Fibre 0g; Sodium 0mg.

Gin and lemon fizz

If gin and tonic is your favourite tipple, you'll enjoy this chilled alternative. The fruit and flower ice cubes make a lively decoration for any iced drink.

SERVES 2

mixture of small edible berries or currants,
    pieces of thinly pared lemon or orange rind
tiny edible flowers
4 scoops of Lemon Sorbet
30ml/2 tbsp gin
about 120ml/4fl oz/$^1/_2$ cup chilled tonic water

1 To make the decorated ice cubes, place each fruit, piece of rind or flower in a section of an ice cube tray. Carefully fill with water and freeze for several hours until the cubes are solid.

2 Divide the sorbet among two cocktail glasses or, alternatively, use small tumblers, with a capacity of about 150ml/$^1/_4$ pint/$^2/_3$ cup.

3 Spoon over the gin and add a couple of the ornamental ice cubes to each glass. Top up with tonic water and serve immediately.

COOK'S TIP
When making the ice cubes, choose small herb flowers such as borage or mint, or edible flowers such as rose geraniums, primulas or rosebuds.

Nutritional information per portion: Energy 119kcal/504kJ; Protein 0.5g; Carbohydrate 22.4g, of which sugars 17.1g; Fat 0g, of which saturates 0g; Cholesterol 0mg; Calcium 2mg; Fibre 0g; Sodium 12mg.

Iced mango lassi

Based on a traditional Indian drink, this iced yogurt drink is excellent with spicy food, and makes an excellent alcohol-free cocktail and welcome cooler at any time of day.

SERVES 3–4

FOR THE YOGURT ICE
175g/6oz/³/₄ cup caster
   (superfine) sugar
150ml/¹/₄ pint/²/₃ cup water
2 lemons
500ml/17fl oz/generous 2 cups Greek
   (strained plain) yogurt

FOR EACH DRINK
120ml/4fl oz/¹/₂ cup mango juice
2–3 ice cubes (optional)
fresh mint sprigs and wedges of mango,
   to serve

1 Gently heat the sugar and water in a pan, stirring occasionally, until the sugar dissolves. Leave to cool in a jug, then chill until very cold. Grate the lemon rinds and add with the juice to the chilled syrup and stir well to mix.

2 Pour the syrup mixture into a container and freeze until thickened. Beat in the yogurt and return to the freezer until thick enough to scoop.

3 To make each lassi, briefly blend the mango juice with three small scoops of the yogurt ice in a food processor or blender until just smooth. Pour the mixture into a tall glass or tumbler and add the ice cubes, if using. Top each drink with another scoop of the yogurt ice and decorate. Serve at once.

Nutritional information per portion: Energy 366kcal/1546kJ; Protein 8.8g; Carbohydrate 60.6g, of which sugars 60.3g; Fat 12.9g, of which saturates 6.6g; Cholesterol 0mg; Calcium 221mg; Fibre 2.3g; Sodium 93mg.

Tropical fruit sodas

For many children, scoops of vanilla ice cream served in a froth of lemonade would make the perfect treat. This more elaborate version will appeal to adults too.

SERVES 4

10ml/2 tsp sugar
1 papaya
1 small ripe mango
2 passion fruit
8 large scoops of Classic Vanilla ice cream
8 large scoops of Banana and Toffee ice cream
about 400ml/14fl oz/1²/₃ cups chilled lemonade or soda water

1 Line a baking sheet with foil. Make four small mounds of sugar on the foil, using about 2.5ml/¹/₂ tsp each time, spacing them well apart. Lightly grill (broil) until the sugar mounds have turned to a pale golden caramel. Then swirl them with the tip of a cocktail stick for a feathery finish. Leave to cool.

2 Cut the papaya in half. Scoop out the seeds, remove the skin and chop the flesh. Skin the mango and chop it into bitesize chunks. Mix both in a bowl. Cut each passion fruit in half and scoop the pulp into the bowl of fruit. Mix well, cover and chill until ready to serve.

3 Divide the chilled fruit mixture among four large tumblers of about 300ml/¹/₂ pint/1¹/₄ cups capacity. Add one scoop of each type of ice cream to each glass. Peel the caramel decorations carefully away from the foil and press gently into the ice cream. Top up with lemonade or soda and serve.

Nutritional information per portion: Energy 504kcal/2106kJ; Protein 8.4g; Carbohydrate 56.6g, of which sugars 56.3g; Fat 28.6g, of which saturates 17g; Cholesterol 0mg; Calcium 228mg; Fibre 4g; Sodium 128mg.

Lemonade on ice

Home-made lemonade may not fizz, but its fresh, tangy flavour is unmatched by bought drinks. The basic lemonade will keep well in the fridge for up to two weeks.

SERVES 6

6 lemons
225g/8oz/1 cup caster (superfine) sugar
1.75 litres/3 pints/7½ cups boiling water

FOR EACH ICED DRINK

4 scoops of Lemon Sorbet
thin lemon and lime slices
3 ice cubes, crushed
mint sprigs and halved lemon and
    lime slices, to decorate

1 Start by making the lemonade. Wash the lemons and dry them thoroughly. Pare all the lemons thinly, avoiding the bitter white pith, and put the rind in a large heatproof bowl. Add the sugar. Squeeze the lemons and set the juice aside.

2 Pour the measured boiling water over the lemon rinds and sugar. Stir until the sugar dissolves. Leave to cool, then stir in the lemon juice. Strain the lemonade into a large jug and chill.

3 For each glass of iced lemonade, place four scoops of sorbet in a tall glass and tuck some lemon and lime slices down the sides. Add the crushed ice. Top up each glass with about 200ml/7fl oz/scant 1 cup of the lemonade. Decorate with mint and halved lemon and lime slices.

Nutritional information per portion: Energy 171kcal/729kJ; Protein 0.4g; Carbohydrate 45.2g, of which sugars 45.2g; Fat 0g, of which saturates 0g; Cholesterol 0mg; Calcium 21mg; Fibre 0g; Sodium 6mg.

Cranberry, cinnamon and ginger spritzer

Partially freezing fruit juice gives it a wonderfully slushy texture that is very refreshing. The combination of cranberry and apple juices produces a tart, clean flavour that's not too sweet.

SERVES 4

600ml/1 pint/2¹/₂ cups chilled
    cranberry juice
150ml/¹/₄ pint/²/₃ cup clear apple juice
4 cinnamon sticks
about 400ml/14fl oz/1²/₃ cups chilled
    ginger ale
a few fresh or frozen cranberries,
    to decorate

1 Freeze the cranberry juice in a shallow freezerproof container for 2 hours or until a thick layer of ice crystals has formed around the edges. Then mash with a fork to break up the ice, then return the mixture to the freezer for a further 2–3 hours until almost solid.

2 Pour the apple juice into a small pan, add 2 cinnamon sticks and bring to just below boiling point. Pour into a jug and leave to cool, then remove the cinnamon sticks and set them aside with the other cinnamon sticks. Chill the juice until it is very cold.

3 Spoon the cranberry ice into a food processor. Add the apple juice and blend very briefly until slushy. Pile into cocktail glasses or flutes, top up with chilled ginger ale and decorate with the fresh or frozen cranberries. Pop a long cinnamon stick into each glass, to use as a swizzle stick.

Nutritional information per portion: Energy 86kcal/370kJ; Protein 0.2g; Carbohydrate 22.5g, of which sugars 22.5g; Fat 0.2g, of which saturates 0g; Cholesterol 0mg; Calcium 13mg; Fibre 0g; Sodium 4mg.

Snowball

For many of us, a "snowball" is a Christmas indulgence. This iced version, enhanced with melting vanilla ice cream, lime and nutmeg, may just tempt you to drink advocaat on other occasions too.

SERVES 4

8 scoops of Classic Vanilla ice cream
120ml/4fl oz/1/2 cup advocaat
60ml/4 tbsp freshly squeezed lime juice
freshly grated nutmeg
about 300ml/1/2 pint/11/4 cups chilled lemonade

1 Put half the vanilla ice cream in a food processor or blender and add the advocaat and the lime juice, with plenty of freshly grated nutmeg. Process the mixture briefly until well combined.

2 Scoop the remaining ice cream into four medium tumblers. Spoon over the advocaat mixture and top up the glasses with lemonade. Sprinkle with more nutmeg and serve immediately.

COOK'S TIP
Freshly grated nutmeg has a warm, nutty aroma and flavour that works as well in creamy drinks as it does in sweet and savoury dishes. A small nutmeg grater is a worthwhile investment if you don't have one.

Nutritional information per portion: Energy 329kcal/1369kJ; Protein 3.9g; Carbohydrate 28g, of which sugars 27.9g; Fat 19.8g, of which saturates 9.1g; Cholesterol 0mg; Calcium 109mg; Fibre 0g; Sodium 92mg.

Strawberry daiquiri

Based on the classic cocktail, this version is a wonderful drink which retains the essential ingredients of rum and lime and combines them with fresh strawberries and strawberry ice cream to create a thick iced fruit purée.

SERVES 4

225g/8oz/2 cups strawberries, hulled
5ml/1 tsp caster (superfine) sugar
120ml/4fl oz/1/2 cup Bacardi rum
30ml/2 tbsp freshly squeezed lime juice
8 scoops of Simple Strawberry ice cream
about 150ml/1/4 pint/2/3 cup chilled lemonade
extra strawberries and lime slices, to decorate

1 Blend the strawberries with the sugar in a food processor or blender, then press the purée through a sieve (strainer) into a bowl. Return the strawberry purée to the blender with the rum, lime juice and half the strawberry ice cream. Blend until smooth.

2 Scoop the remaining strawberry ice cream into four cocktail glasses or small tumblers and pour over the blended mixture.

3 Top up with lemonade, decorate with fresh strawberries and lime slices, and serve.

Nutritional information per portion: Energy 189kcal/789kJ; Protein 0.6g; Carbohydrate 19.8g, of which sugars 19.8g; Fat 0.1g, of which saturates 0g; Cholesterol 0mg; Calcium 19mg; Fibre 0.8g; Sodium 5mg.

Ice cream basics

Making ice cream at home is surprisingly simple, needs little equipment and is enormously satisfying. Covering the essential aspects of making ices in all their rich variety, as well as sauces, cones, biscuits and decorations, this chapter outlines the skills and techniques necessary for even the most ambitious and elaborate iced desserts.

Essential equipment

You will probably already have most of what you need to make ice creams and ices. Real enthusiasts, however, may want to invest in a free-standing electric ice cream maker.

THE BASICS FOR MAKING ICES

Making ices by hand is the simplest method of all, and is known as "still freezing". All you need are glass bowls, a fork, a manual or electric hand-held whisk for beating and a freezerproof container with a lid. You will also need a heavy pan for making the custard, sugar syrups and cooking fruits, plus a sieve (strainer) for puréeing and a lemon squeezer and fine grater for citrus fruits.

A food processor is a useful aid for breaking down the ice crystals, although it can be wasteful of ingredients. However, this method does produce a similar texture to that made in an electric ice cream maker.

ABOVE: *For large quantities, a hand-held electric whisk saves time and adds volume.*

For storage

You will need freezerproof containers of varying sizes, with tight-fitting lids to eliminate the transfer of strong smells and flavours and prevent the surface of the ice cream from drying out. Use containers a little larger than the quantity of ice cream, to allow for beating during freezing and increased volume when frozen. A headspace of 2cm/³⁄₄in is adequate. Granita is the exception, as it requires as shallow a container as possible to reduce freezing time. Use ONLY stainless steel or aluminium while making ice cream or sorbet as other metals can impart a metallic taste.

The freezer

An upright or chest domestic freezer is essential. To make ice cream, the temperature should be -18°C/-66°F. A freezer thermometer is a very useful tool. The colder the freezer, the more quickly the ice freezes, making smaller ice crystals and smoother ice cream. If the freezer is badly packed, the motor has to work harder to maintain temperature.

ICE CREAM MAKERS

There are two basic types: those with a built-in freezing unit; and those with a detachable double-skinned bowl, which must be pre-frozen before use. There are also machines that can be run inside a standard freezer. These have very poor motors and you can generally get better results by hand.

The most efficient – and most expensive – models have an integral freezing unit. Motors vary, depending

ABOVE: *An ice cream maker with integral motor and freezing unit.*

on the manufacturer, so if you are buying one, choose the most powerful motor. If possible, see it in action, as noise levels vary greatly. As this type are often larger than a food processor, working and storage space are prime considerations. They come with two bowls: a stainless-steel bowl built into the unit; and an aluminium bucket that slots into it. Most have a see-through lid and a vent for adding extra ingredients. This plastic top simply slides off for easy washing.

A PRE-FREEZING ICE CREAM MAKER

For a slightly cheaper option, look out for a model with a detachable double-skinned bowl filled with freezing liquid. This type of machine will need to be frozen for at least 18 hours before use. When you are ready to use the ice cream maker, you simply fit the motor and paddle to the frozen bowl, switch on the power, and fill the bowl with the ice cream or sorbet mixture. It usually takes 25–40 minutes for the ice cream to churn.

If the freezer is large enough, the bowl can be stored there, giving the option to make home-made ice cream at any time. For larger quantities, it is very useful to have a second detachable bowl on stand-by and make two batches of ice cream.

When possible, eat the ice cream soon after it is made to fully enjoy the wonderful texture of fresh machine-made ice cream.

USEFUL EXTRAS
Scoops

There are many ice cream scoops on the market. Choose from brightly coloured plastic scoops with quick release levers, half-moon-shaped stainless-steel scoops with sleek steel handles, simple spoon-shaped scoops with metal handles or easy-grip moulded plastic handles. To be really impressive, use silver scoops.

BELOW: A simple ice cream maker with motorized paddles.

A sugar thermometer

To make parfaits, you will need everything you need to make ices, plus a good sugar thermometer, which, though expensive, ensures perfect results. Choose one with a clip to hold it in place on the pan.

Melon ballers

Ice cream looks very attractive when scooped with a melon baller. Available from good cookshops in varying sizes, from pea to grape size, the larger size is best for ice cream. To make a ball, press the upturned cup into slightly softened ice cream, then rotate it. Arrange in a glass dish or on a plate, with fresh fruits.

Cone moulds

For a really professional finish, it's best to use wooden moulds, which are available only by mail order. You can, however, improvise by making your own cone moulds from foil-covered cardboard.

BELOW: Ice cream scoops come in many different shapes, materials and colours.

ABOVE: This wooden cone mould is a very simple but useful tool for making professional-looking cones.

Kulfi moulds

Freeze and serve Indian-style ice creams in the traditional way using these tapering, cone-shaped kulfi moulds. They are available from some large Indian supermarkets and other outlets. You can also use lolly moulds, dariole moulds or plastic cups.

BELOW: Making kulfi is easy with a specially designed, all-in-one kulfi mould.

Basic ingredients

By starting with our basic suggestions and adapting them, you will soon create your own repertoire, using only the ingredients that you want.

ICE CREAM
Cream
Whipping cream makes the best ice cream, especially when mixed with coffee, toffee or chocolate. Double (heavy) cream is a must for vanilla or brown bread ice cream. Clotted cream and crème fraîche perfectly complement fruit, honey and spice ice creams. However, the high butter-fat content of double or clotted cream can produce a buttery flavour and texture, especially if overchurned. Avoid UHT creams, as the flavour is so strong.

Milk
Avoid skimmed milk. While it is a healthier option, its low fat content produces a "thin" taste. It is difficult, though, to distinguish between semi-skimmed (low-fat) or full-fat (whole) milk, especially when they are mixed with cream. Full-fat, semi-skimmed and goat's milk all make delicious ice cream.

Yogurt
Some people love yogurt in ice cream; others hate it. Start with mild, creamy, bio-style natural (plain) yogurt before progressing to the sharper sheep's and goat's milk yogurts.

Cheeses
Light, virtually fat-free fromage frais (low-fat cream cheese) can be added to fruit or vanilla ice creams. Italian ricotta is like a cross between cottage and cream cheese and is ideal for certain ice creams. For the richest

ABOVE: *Italian mascarpone makes for rich-tasting fruit and vanilla ice creams.*

results, you can also try mascarpone, another Italian cheese with a deep-buttery yellow colour and a similar texture to cream cheese. Try mixing mascarpone with fromage frais for a rich-tasting, reduced-fat dessert.

Non-dairy products
Sweetened or unsweetened soya milk and canned coconut milk are ideal for vegans or people on a milk-free diet. Coconut milk is also great mixed with lime or lemon.

Eggs
Where possible, use new-laid, organic eggs for the best colour and flavour. They make a big difference to the end product.

Sweeteners
Caster sugar (superfine) is used in the majority of the recipes in this book, as its fine crystals dissolve quickly in the custard, giving a smooth, silky texture. Granulated (white) sugar is used for making the praline, a delicious ingredient in some of the speciality

ABOVE: *Many varieties of milk can be used to make excellent ice cream.*

ABOVE: *Light, refreshing ricotta is just perfect for some ice creams.*

ABOVE: *Muscovado sugar can be a delicious sweetener for ice cream.*

ices, while light and dark-brown muscovado (molasses) sugar are used in some recipes, where the darker colour and stronger flavour is used to to great effect. Honey and maple syrup make delicious additions, on their own or mixed with caster sugar, particularly for ice creams flavoured with nuts.

Cornflour

Many purists are horrified at the thought of using cornflour (cornstarch) in ice cream, arguing that it is far better to make the custard in a double boiler or a large heatproof bowl over simmering water Certainly, it is not a standard ingredient in classic custard, though it does help to stabilize the custard and reduces the risk of curdling. Custard containing a little cornflour is easier to handle and can be cooked gently in a heavy pan. It thickens in 4–5 minutes, compared to at least 15 minutes in a double boiler.

WATER ICES
Sugar syrup

Make a simple sugar syrup by heating caster sugar and water in a medium pan, stirring until the sugar dissolves – there is no need to boil the syrup. Caster sugar is used for syrups in the recipes in this book because it dissolves very rapidly, but granulated (white) sugar can also be used, as can light brown sugar or honey. Once made and cooled, the syrup can be refrigerated for several days.

Flavouring

Choose from a wide range of fresh fruit purées, including strawberry, raspberry, peach, pineapple, passion fruit, mango and lime. Dried fruits are sometimes steeped in apple juice, grape juice, water and brandy or a liqueur mixture before being puréed. You can also infuse citrus rinds (orange, lemon or lime) in the hot syrup for extra flavour and add fresh juice to intensify. Spice infusions or mixtures of spices and fruits create unusual ices that appeal greatly to people with not such a sweet tooth.

ABOVE: *Honey can be used as a sweetener on its own or with sugar.*

Egg white

Adding egg white to a semi-frozen sorbet serves two purposes. Firstly, it helps to stabilize the mixture, which is important for sorbets that melt quickly. Secondly, it can also lighten very dense or fibrous sorbets, such as those made from blackcurrants or blackberries. Egg white requires only minimum beating with a fork to loosen it and need not be beaten until frothy or standing in peaks.

How to separate an egg

Crack the egg on the side of a bowl. Gently ease the halves apart, keeping the yolk in one half and letting the white fall into the bowl. Separate any remaining egg white from the yolk by swapping the yolk from one shell half to the other. Do this several times if necessary, until all the egg white has fallen into the bowl and what remains is the pure egg yolk.

Making ice cream

Many classic ice creams are based on a simple custard made from eggs and milk. It is not difficult to make, but as it is used so frequently, it is worth perfecting by following these very simple guidelines.

MAKING THE CUSTARD BASE

flavouring to infuse (optional)
300ml/¹/₂ pint/1¹/₄ cups semi-skimmed (low-fat) milk
4 medium egg yolks
75g/3oz/6 tbsp caster (superfine) sugar
5ml/1 tsp cornflour (cornstarch)

1 **By hand**: Prepare any flavourings. Split vanilla pods (beans) with a sharp knife; crack coffee beans with a mallet. You can use cinnamon sticks, whole cloves, fresh rosemary, lavender sprigs and bay leaves as they are.

2 Pour the milk into a pan. Bring it to the boil, then remove the pan from the heat, add the chosen flavouring and leave to infuse for 30 minutes or until cool.

3 If you have used a vanilla pod, lift it out of the pan, and using a small, sharp knife, scrape the seeds back into the milk to enrich the flavour. Whisk the egg yolks, caster sugar and cornflour in a bowl until thick and foamy. Bring the plain or infused milk to the boil, then gradually whisk it into the yolk mixture. Pour the combined mixture back into the pan.

4 Cook the custard mixture over a low heat, stirring constantly until it approaches boiling point and thickens to the point where the custard will coat the back of a wooden spoon. Do not let it overheat or it may curdle. Then take the pan off the heat and continue stirring, making sure that you take the spoon right around the bottom edges of the pan.

5 Pour the custard into a bowl and cover the surface with clear film (plastic wrap) to prevent the formation of a skin, or cover the surface with a light sprinkling of caster sugar. Leave to cool, then chill until required.

6 **Using an ice cream maker**: Follow steps 1–5 as above but ensure the custard is chilled before starting.

Rescuing curdled custard
Quickly take the pan off the heat and plunge it into a sink half filled with cold water. Stir frequently, taking the spoon right into the bottom edges of the pan. Keep stirring for 4–5 minutes until the temperature of the custard has dropped and the custard has stabilized. You may also find it helpful to whisk the mixture. If all else fails, sieve it.

USING FLAVOURINGS

1 By hand: If you haven't infused the milk, you may wish to flavour the custard. To make chocolate custard, stir pieces of white, dark (bittersweet) or milk chocolate into the hot custard in the pan, off the heat. Stir occasionally for 5 minutes until the chocolate has melted completely. Pour the flavoured custard into a bowl, and then cover and cool. Chill in the refrigerator.

2 Add other flavourings such as strong coffee (either filter or instant dissolved in boiling water), flower waters such as orange flower water or rose water and sweeteners that also add flavour, such as maple syrup or honey. Vanilla, peppermint and almond extract are popular flavourings. You should add these to the custard after it has cooled.

ADDING CREAM

1 Using an ice cream maker: If you are making ice cream in an ice cream maker, make sure that you always follow the preliminary instructions for your specific machine, pre-cooling the machine or chilling the bowl in the freezer. Stir whipping cream, whipped double (heavy) cream or any soft cream cheeses into the chilled plain or flavoured custard and then churn until firm.

2 Creams with a high fat proportion – double cream, clotted cream or crème fraîche – should only be added to ice creams that are partially frozen, as they have a tendency to become buttery if churned for too long. Double cream can sometimes be added at the start of the process, but only for small quantities and minimal churning times.

By hand: Make the ice cream by hand in a freezerproof container by folding soft whipped cream into the chilled plain or flavoured custard and pouring into the tub. Allow enough space for beating the ice cream during freezing. Crème fraîche, clotted cream and cream cheeses can also be added at this stage.

Fruit and cream combinations
The combination of custard, cream and fruit purée can sometimes be too rich and just dulls the fruit flavour. So you can just use sieved (strained) fresh berry fruit, purées or poached and puréed orchard fruits stirred into whipped cream. If using an ice cream maker, partially freezing the purée before stirring in the cream speeds up the churning time.

MAKING A BASIC PARFAIT

Made correctly, a parfait is a light, cream-based confection with a softer, smoother texture than ice cream. It does not need beating during freezing, so is ideal for anyone who does not have an electric ice cream maker.

Parfaits can be set in moulds, tall glasses, china dishes or chocolate cups. The secret lies in the sugar syrup. Dissolve the sugar gently without stirring so that it does not crystallize, then boil rapidly until it registers 119°C/238°F on a sugar thermometer. This is the soft ball stage.

Quickly whisk the syrup into the whisked eggs. Cook over hot water until very thick. Cool, then mix with flavourings, alcohol and whipped cream. Freeze until solid and serve straight from the freezer.

Other flavourings

Usually made with coffee, parfaits are also delicious made with ground spices such as cinnamon with apple or ginger with banana. Double (heavy) cream adds richness, and crème fraîche and whipping cream are good too. Or, for something more sophisticated, try fruit purées mixed with Kirsch, Cointreau or Grand Marnier.

SERVES FOUR

115g/4oz/generous ½ cup caster (superfine) sugar
120ml/4fl oz/½ cup water
4 medium egg yolks
flavourings
300ml/½ pint/1¼ cups double (heavy) cream

1 Gently heat the sugar and water in a pan, without stirring, until the sugar dissolves. Half fill a medium pan with water and bring to simmering point.

2 Bring the sugar syrup to the boil and boil rapidly for 4–5 minutes until it starts to thicken. It will be ready to use when it registers 119°C/238°F on a sugar thermometer, or forms a soft ball when dropped into water.

3 Whisk the eggs in a heatproof bowl until frothy. Place over the simmering water and gradually whisk in the hot sugar syrup. Whisk steadily until creamy. Take off the heat. Whisk until cool and the whisk leaves a trail across the surface when lifted.

4 Fold in the chosen flavourings, such as melted chocolate and brandy, ground cinnamon and coffee, whisky

and chopped ginger, Kirsch and raspberry purée or kir and strawberry purèe. In a separate bowl, whip the cream lightly until it just holds its shape. Fold it into the mixture.

5 Pour the parfait mixture into moulds, dishes or chocolate-lined cases. Freeze for at least 4 hours or until firm. Decorate, if liked, with whipped cream, spoonfuls of crème fraîche, chocolate-dipped fruits or caramel shapes. Serve immediately.

BOILING SUGAR

1 If you don't have a thermometer, check whether the sugar syrup is at the soft ball stage by lowering a spoon into it and lifting it up. If the syrup falls steadily from the spoon, it is not ready. Cook for a little longer.

2 The syrup is ready to test when it looks tacky and forms pliable strands when two spoons are dipped in it, back to back, and then pulled apart.

Take the pan off the heat and test by dropping a little boiling syrup into a bowl of iced water. It should form a solidified ball. Wait a few seconds until it cools, then lift it out. You should be able to mould it with your fingertips.

3 Once the syrup has reached soft ball stage, prevent it overcooking by plunging the base of the pan into cold water – either in a sink or in a shallow container. If the syrup is allowed to overcook, it will crystallize in the pan, forming brittle, glass-like strands, which snap. Adding over-cooked syrup to the eggs will cause the mixture to solidify into a rock-solid mass that is impossible to mix.

FREEZING ICE CREAM

Freezing is a crucial stage in the making of home-made ice cream and there are two basic freezing methods: "still freezing" (freezing without a machine); and "stir freezing" (using an ice cream maker). Making ice cream by hand today requires freezing it in a tub or similar container and beating it several times during the freezing process. This process is all done automatically in an ice cream maker.

The secret of a really good ice cream is minute ice crystals. The finished ice cream should be light and cold but not icy. If the crystals are large, the ice cream will have a grainy, coarse texture, which will detract from the taste. Beating the ice cream, either by hand or with an ice cream maker, breaks down the crystals. The more it is beaten while it is freezing, the finer and silkier the finished texture.

FREEZING WITH AN ICE CREAM MAKER

1 Prepare your ice cream maker according to the manufacturer's instructions. Then pour the chilled custard and whipping cream into the bowl, fit the paddle, fix on the lid and begin churning.

2 After 10–15 minutes of churning, the ice cream will have begun to freeze. The mixture will thicken and will start to look slushy. Continue to churn in the same way.

3 After 20–25 minutes of churning, the ice cream will be considerably thicker but still too soft to scoop. This is the ideal time to mix in any of your chosen additional flavourings such as praline, liqueurs, purées or browned breadcrumbs.

ABOVE: *Electric machines take a lot of the hard work out of making ice cream.*

Making water ices

Sorbets, like water ices, are made with a light sugar syrup flavoured with fruit juice, fruit purée, wine, liqueur, tea or herbs. They should not contain milk or cream, and are best made in an ice cream maker, as the constant churning ensures that the ice crystals are as tiny as possible, for a smoother texture.

MAKING A BASIC SORBET
SERVES 6

150–200g/5–7oz/³/₄–1 cup caster
   (superfine) sugar
200–300ml/7–10fl oz/³/₄–1¹/₄ cups water
flavouring
1 egg white

1 Put the sugar and water in a medium pan and heat the mixture, stirring, until the sugar just dissolves.

2 Add pared citrus rinds, herbs or spices, depending on your chosen flavouring. Leave to infuse. Strain and cool, then chill well in the fridge.

3 Mix with additional flavourings such as fruit juices, strained puréed fruits, herbs or tea.

4 Using an ice cream maker: Pour the syrup mixture into the machine and churn until it is thick but still too soft to scoop.

5 Lightly beat the egg white with a fork and pour it into the ice cream maker, either through the top vent or by removing the lid completely, depending on the make. Continue churning until the sorbet is firm enough to scoop with a spoon.

Making fruit purées
As an approximate guide, 500g/1¹/₄lb/5 cups of berry fruits will produce about 450ml/³/₄ pint/scant 2 cups purée. Mix this with 115g–150g/4–5oz/generous

6 By hand: Pour the mixture into a plastic tub or similar freezerproof container. It should not be more than 4cm/1¹/₂in deep. Cover and freeze in the coldest part of the freezer for 4 hours or until it has partially frozen and ice crystals have begun to form. Beat until smooth with a fork, or hand-held electric whisk. Alternatively, process in a food processor until smooth.

7 Lightly beat the egg white and stir it into the sorbet. Freeze until firm enough to scoop (about 4 hours).

¹/₂–³/₄ cup caster (superfine) sugar (depending on natural acidity), dissolved in 300ml/¹/₂ pint/1¹/₄ cups boiling water and made up to 1 litre/1³/₄ pints/4 cups with extra cold water, lemon or lime juice.

GRANITAS
Citrus granita

This wonderfully refreshing, simple Italian-style water ice has the fine texture of snow and is most often served piled into pretty glass dishes. You don't need fancy or expensive equipment, just a medium pan, a sieve (strainer) or blender for puréeing the fruit, a fork and room in the freezer for a large plastic container.

Ingredients

There are no hard-and-fast rules when it comes to the proportions of sugar to water, nor is there a standard amount of flavouring which must be added. Unlike sorbets, granitas consist largely of water, with just enough sugar to sweeten them and prevent them from freezing too hard. A total of 1 litre/1¾ pints/4 cups of flavoured sugar syrup will provide six generous portions of granita.

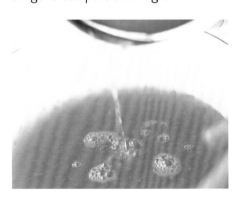

1 Juice six lemons, oranges or four ruby (pink) grapefruit. Add 115–200g/4–7oz/generous ½–1 cup caster (superfine) sugar (the precise amount depends on the fruit's natural acidity). Dissolve the sugar in 300ml/½ pint/1¼ cups boiling water, then mix it with the citrus juice

and rind. Top up to 1 litre/1¾ pints/4 cups with extra water or water and alcohol. Add enough alcohol to taste but don't be too generous or the granita will not freeze.

2 Pour the chilled mixture into a large plastic tub or similar freezerproof container. It should not be more than 2–2.5cm/¾–1in deep. Freeze in the coldest part of the freezer for 2 hours until it is mushy around the edges.

Remove from the freezer and beat well with a fork to break up the ice crystals. Return to the freezer. Beat at 30 minute intervals for 2 hours until it has the texture of snow.

Making a hot infusion

Some of the most delicious granitas are based on hot mixtures. Coffee is just one example. Pour hot, strong filtered coffee into a bowl or pan and stir in sugar to taste. For a ginger granita, infuse finely chopped fresh root ginger in boiling water, then sweeten it. Chocolate granita is made by mixing unsweetened cocoa powder to a smooth paste with a little boiling water and sweetening to taste. All hot infusions must be left to cool, then chilled in the fridge before being frozen.

Fruit-flavoured granita

To make a fruit-flavoured granita, purée berry fruits such as raspberries or strawberries, then sieve (strain) to remove the seeds. Alternatively, purée ripe peaches, then sieve to remove the skins. To make a melon granita, scoop the seeds out of orange- or green-fleshed melons, then purée the flesh. Peeled and seeded watermelon can be puréed in the same way, or the flesh can be puréed along with the seeds and then strained afterwards.

ABOVE: *After puréeing fruits, always strain them to remove the skin and seeds.*

Serving and storing granitas

Coffee granita is classically served in a tumbler with whipped cream on top. Other types look pretty in tall glasses and decorated with fresh fruits, herb leaves and flowers. Because of its soft texture, a granita is best served as soon as it is made. Or, try leaving it for a couple of hours in the freezer, beating once or twice more. If you must freeze one overnight, or longer, let it thaw slightly and beat really well with a fork before serving. The ice crystals will be smaller but the taste will be the same.

Flavourings

Spices and herbs, from sweet and sharp to aromatic and fragranced, fruits of every kind and flower waters can all be used to flavour ice creams, ices and sorbets (sherbets). Try experimenting to discover what you like best.

HERBS AND FLOWERS
Edible flowers

A sprinkling of just a few petals or tiny flower heads from the garden can turn even a few simple scoops of home-made strawberry or vanilla ice cream into a dinner party dessert. A few vibrant pansies, tiny violas mixed with primrose petals or dainty violets are perfect for spring decorations, while rose petals, borage flowers, elderflowers, cicely flowers or sprigs of lavender are ideal in summer. For something bolder, use yellow or orange marigold petals (but not French marigolds) or nasturtiums. Beware though: not all flowers are edible. Avoid any plants grown from bulbs or not found in a herb garden.

Flower waters

A few drops of orange flower, orange blossom water or rose water add a delicate fragrance to ground almond or summer berry ices and sorbets.

Herbs

Rosemary, bay, mint and lavender are great with creamy ice creams, sherbets or sorbets. Infuse a few sprigs of rosemary or lavender, two to three whole bay leaves or a small bunch of fresh mint in cream or freshly boiled sugar syrup. Leave to cool, then strain. Add a little fresh chopped mint or other herbs to finished ice creams or sorbets.

SPICES
Ginger

Perfect with tropical fruit, ginger also gives a glorious lift to rhubarb- or pear-flavoured ices. Preserved stem ginger, ginger syrup and ginger wine make delicious ice cream sauces.

Peel fresh root ginger, then slice or chop thinly. Or, grate it with a fine-tooth grater. Slice or chop preserved stem ginger; finely chop large pieces of candied or crystallized ginger.

ABOVE: *It is easiest to grate ginger when frozen. It thaws instantly on being grated.*

Vanilla

Delicious in ice cream, whipped cream and custard, vanilla is available as seed pods (beans), vanilla sugar and vanilla extract. Good-quality extract is labelled "natural vanilla extract".

Slit the whole vanilla pod (bean), add it to freshly boiled cream or milk, leave to cool and infuse. Holding the pod over the pan, scrape the tiny black seeds with a small knife into the cream or milk for excellent ice cream. Keep the pods, rinse under cold water, pat dry with kitchen paper and store two or three in a jar of caster sugar to make your own vanilla sugar. Vanilla extract is highly concentrated, so use only 2.5–5ml/$\frac{1}{2}$–1 tsp for ice cream.

ABOVE: *Lavender is an ideal decoration for ices during the summer months.*

ABOVE: *To peel fresh root ginger, use a vegetable peeler or small, sharp knife.*

ABOVE: *Use a knife to scrape the seeds from a vanilla pod into milk or cream.*

ABOVE: *Cinnamon works well with nectarine and peach recipes.*

Cinnamon

This gentle spice is obtained from the bark of the cinnamon tree, which is native to India. You can buy cinnamon as dried sticks or quills, or as finely ground spice (which, however, is seldom used in ice creams, except as a decoration). Cinnamon adds a delicious flavour to ice creams made with peaches or nectarines.

Infuse halved cinnamon sticks in freshly boiled milk or cream. When it has imparted its flavour, strain and use the milk or cream to make the custard base for ice cream. Cinnamon sticks can also be used to infuse fruit purées or compotes in the same way.

ABOVE: *Commonly associated with hot dishes, cardamom adds flavour to ices too.*

Nutmeg

Available either whole or ground, nutmeg complements both sweet and savoury dishes, and is delicious in ice creams. You can buy blades of mace, the pretty orange outer coating, separately, and both are sold ground.

To get the best flavour, grate a little off a whole nutmeg as needed. Use a small nutmeg grater or the fine-toothed surface of an ordinary grater. Ready-ground nutmeg rapidly loses its pungency when stored.

Cardamom

Although traditionally used in Indian, Arabian and North African cooking, cardamom also adds a delicate and aromatic fragrance to sorbets, ice creams and fruit compotes.

If the recipe calls for cardamom seeds, crush the pods with the back of a knife until they split and remove any remaining seeds with the tip. Use both the pod and the seeds for maximum flavour.

Cloves

Available whole or ground, cloves are widely used in desserts, particularly with apples and other fruits. Although pungent, they add an intriguing flavour to ice creams if used sparingly, but don't overdo it.

Infuse whole cloves in milk or cream, especially when making a custard base for a fruit ice cream.

Lemon grass

Once considerd a little exotic, delicately fragranced lemon grass is now widely available as fresh pale-

ABOVE: *It is always best to grate nutmeg fresh, as and when you need it.*

green, white-tipped stems, or as dried whole stems. It is also sold ground in jars. To extract the flavour, soak dried stems in warm water for at least two hours before use. Fresh lemon grass can be finely sliced or crushed and infused in the milk to be used for custard-based ice cream, or infused in the sugar syrup for a granita or sorbet.

Star anise

These star-shaped pods are a favourite with Chinese cooks but are now more popular in the West. Use them for sauces and compotes or infuse them in sugar syrups or custards for ices with a lovely aniseed flavour.

ABOVE: *Star anise adds aniseed flavour to sugar syrups and custards.*

Chocolate

White or dark, strong or sweet, chocolate is an ice cream essential. But the best results depend on using the highest-quality ingredients.

CHOOSING FOR FLAVOUR

A strong chocolate is vital when making ice cream and, basically, the higher the cocoa solids, the stronger the chocolate flavour. So avoid any chocolate with less than 45 per cent cocoa solids. Plain (semisweet) dessert chocolate contains between 30 and 60 per cent. For a quality dark (bittersweet) or bitter chocolate, choose a "luxury" or "Belgian" variety, as it will almost certainly have at least 75 per cent cocoa solids. You can also use chocolate Menier, which is less sweet with a stronger flavour.

Avoid chocolate cake coverings, as they have less chocolate taste and are more suitable for chocolate curls or caraque. However, you can mix cake covering with an equal quantity of luxury dark chocolate. The melting and moulding qualities of one combine with the superior taste of the other.

ABOVE: *A strong chocolate, high in cocoa solids, is a must when making ice cream.*

Couverture

This pure chocolate is available as white, milk and dark or as a block, and contains no fats other than cocoa butter. It is used mainly by professionals and only available from specialist suppliers. It generally requires "tempering" before use to distribute the cocoa fat evenly. This is quite a lengthy process that involves warming and working the chocolate until it reaches 32°C/90°F. Couverture is usually used for moulding or decorating because of its glossy finish.

ABOVE: *Couverture, the professionals' choice, usually needs tempering before use.*

White chocolate

As when buying dark chocolate, always choose "luxury" or "Swiss" white chocolate for the best flavour. White chocolate is made from cocoa butter extracted during the production of cocoa solids. Although it includes about 2 per cent cocoa solids, many purists argue that this is not nearly enough to make it a true chocolate, especially as the cocoa butter is then mixed with milk solids, sugar and flavourings.

ABOVE: *Always choose white chocolate with at least 25 per cent cocoa butter.*

As a result, it requires extra care when being melted: it quickly hardens if overheated. Check the pack before buying and choose a brand with a minimum of 25 per cent cocoa butter, as any chocolate with less will be difficult to melt. The more cocoa butter there is, the creamier and softer the chocolate. Some brands may even include vegetable fat or oils, so always check the ingredients list.

Cocoa

This rich, strong, dark powder is made by extracting some of the cocoa butter during chocolate production. What remains is a block containing, on average, 20 per cent cocoa butter, though this varies with each manufacturer. The cocoa is then ground and mixed with sugar and starch. The addition of starch means it needs to be cooked briefly to remove the raw, floury taste. This can be done by mixing it to a paste with a little boiling water. If the cocoa is intended for a sauce, it will probably be mixed with hot milk.

ABOVE: *Milk chocolate has a lower cocoa solid content than dark chocolate and, as a result, a milder flavour. Therefore, add more if using it to flavour ice cream.*

The Netherlands is considered to produce the very best cocoa. It is alkalized through a process devised by the manufacturer Van Houten about 150 years ago. Although more expensive than other brands, Dutch cocoa is definitely worth using for ice cream and chocolate sauces.

Milk chocolate

Mild and creamy, milk chocolate is made with up to 40 per cent milk or milk products, and contains less cocoa solids than dark chocolate. Because it has a mild flavour, you will need to add more than when using dark chocolate. You can use a combination of melted milk chocolate and chopped milk chocolate. As with white chocolate, the addition of milk products mean that it requires more careful heating than dark chocolate.

Carob

Although not a true chocolate, carob is viewed by many as an acceptable alternative. Carob is the ground seedpod of the carob or locust tree and can be used as a substitute. It is usually available from health food shops, and is sold in bars or in a powdered form as flour. If you are using a bar, be careful, as it is highly concentrated. The flour can be used in a similar way to the way you would use unsweetened cocoa powder.

How to melt chocolate

1 Bring a third of a pan of water to the boil, turn the heat off and fit a heatproof bowl over the pan, making sure that the water does not touch the base of the bowl. Break the chocolate into pieces and put it in the bowl.

2 Leave for 4–5 minutes, without stirring, until the chocolate melts. The pieces will hold their shape. Stir briefly before folding into ice cream, or using it as the basis of a sauce.

Storing chocolate

Wrap opened packs well or store in a plastic box, in a cool, dry place away from strong-flavoured foods. Avoid very cold places or the chocolate will develop a whitish bloom. Always check sell-by dates before cooking.

Fruits

We all need to eat more fruit, and there can surely be no better way to enjoy them than in delicious ice creams, sorbets, ices and sauces.

Soft berry fruits

Raspberries, larger tayberries, loganberries, golden raspberries, bright red strawberries, blueberries and blackberries make delicious ice creams, sorbets, sherbets and sauces.

Sprinkle blueberries and red berries over ice cream sundaes or crush them and add to setting ice cream for texture and colour. Use expensive alpine and Hautbois strawberries for decoration only.

To prepare berry fruits, purée them, then press them through a fine sieve (strainer) to remove the seeds.

Cane fruits

Black-, red- and whitecurrants, green gooseberries and red gooseberries all make good ice creams, sherbets, sorbets, coulis and sauces.

ABOVE: *A joy to taste, redcurrants also make beautiful decorations for ice creams.*

Gently remove currants from their stems with a fork. Blackcurrants have a very sharp flavour, so poach them first with sugar and a little water until tender. Lightly poach red- and whitecurrants or eat them raw. Top and tail gooseberries with scissors before cooking, and purée and sieve currants or cooked gooseberries if adding to ice cream, sorbet or sherbet.

Orchard fruits

Apples, pears, plums, damsons, cherries and apricots, peaches and nectarines make irresistible ice creams, sorbets and other desserts.

Peel and core apples and pears, and halve and stone plums, peaches and apricots, poach in a little water and sugar until tender, then process to a smooth purée. Purée ripe peaches, nectarines and apricots raw, and sieve to remove the skins. Poach damsons and scoop out the stones (pits), or press the cooked fruit through a sieve. Use pitted cherries whole or roughly chopped and ripe larger fruits for decoration, sliced or chopped. Toss apples and pears in a little lemon juice to prevent discoloration.

Citrus fruits

Lemons, limes, oranges, tangerines, clementines, kumquats and grapefruits make great sorbets, granitas and sauces. Oranges make great ice cream.

For decoration, grate citrus rinds or pare thinly, removing only the coloured skin, leaving behind the white pith. Cut the fruit in half, squeeze it and strain to remove the pips. Mix it with cream and custard for ice cream, or with

ABOVE: *Lemons, limes and other citrus fruits make sharp, refreshing sorbets.*

sugar syrup for sorbets, sherbets and granitas. Poach kumquats whole or in slices to accompany iced desserts.

Rhubarb

In fact, rhubarb is a vegetable, not a fruit. For iced desserts, choose the early forced rhubarb with its delicate flavour and baby-pink stems. Maincrop rhubarb is coarser with thicker, darker stems. Both must be cooked with sugar and a tablespoon or two of water.

Purée cooked rhubarb for sorbets and granitas, or flavour it with ginger for ice cream. Lightly poached, it is a good accompaniment to vanilla, cinnamon or goat's milk ice cream.

Using dried fruits

Dried sultanas, raisins, prunes, apricots, peaches, dates, figs, mango, cranberries and blueberries are all used in ice creams and sorbets. Dried peaches and apricots produce excellent, intense purées. Use the smaller fruits whole or chopped, steeped in fruit juice, wine, spirits or liqueur. Soak and purée apricots and peaches, before adding to ice cream.

Melons

Canteloupe, Charantais, Galia and Ogen melons make great sorbets and granitas.

Cut them in half, scoop out the seeds, then purée the flesh before use. With watermelons, as the seeds are speckled throughout the flesh, it is easier to leave them in when processing. Straining the purée will remove them. As they have a fairly bland flavour, mix the purée with grated lime rind and juice.

Tropical fruits

Mash peeled bananas or purée them with a little lemon or lime rind to prevent discoloration and make them into ice creams with honey, ginger, chocolate or cinnamon. Puréed or chopped pineapple makes wonderful ice cream, especially with crushed meringue or a few tablespoons of rum. Pineapple can also be puréed and made into sorbets. Mix puréed mango with ginger, lime or coconut for a Caribbean-flavoured sorbet. Grapes and kiwi fruit are best served as accompaniments to iced desserts, although both can be made into sorbets.

ABOVE: *A dash of lemon or lime will prevent bananas discolouring.*

PREPARING A MANGO

1 Place the mango, narrow side down, on a board. Cut a thick, lengthways slice off the sides, keeping the knife blade as close to the central stone as possible. Turn the mango round and repeat on the other side.

2 Make criss-cross cuts in the mango flesh, cutting down only as far as the skin. Then turn the large slices inside out so that the diced flesh stands proud. Scoop it into a bowl.

3 Cut all the remaining fruit away from the stone, remove the skin and dice the flesh.

PREPARING A PASSION FRUIT

Passion fruits are easy to prepare. Just slice them in half and scoop out the fragrant seeds with a teaspoon. If necessary, press the pulp through a sieve (strainer).

PREPARING A PINEAPPLE

To prepare a pineapple, slice the top off, then cut it into slices of the desired width. Cut away the rind with a small sharp knife. Cut away any remaining eyes from the edges of the pineapple slices.

Remove the central core of each slice with an apple corer, pastry cutter or knife.

Glacé (candied) fruits and candied peel

These vibrant, jewel-like fruits make a pretty addition to partially frozen ice cream, and are the traditional flavouring in the classic Italian Tutti Frutti Ice Cream. They can also be used to decorate elaborate ice cream sundaes. Most fruits can be glacéd and a wide selection is available in supermarkets and cookshops. Choose from glacé cherries of various colours, glacé or candied pineapple and candied fruit peels. Large whole or sliced glacé fruits tend to be expensive, but are great for special occasion desserts. Glacé fruits keep well in an airtight container, but are best bought fresh as needed.

Nuts

Subtle, delicate and even slightly savoury, many varieties of nuts can be used to add texture, substance and a wholly satisfying crunch to your home-made ice creams.

A RANGE OF FLAVOURS

Almonds, hazelnuts, pistachios, walnuts, pecans, macadamias, brazil nuts and unsalted peanuts are all used in cream-based ice creams, though rarely in water ices. Ground nuts infused in milk or cream give a delicate flavour to ice creams inspired by the Middle East.

Add finely ground almonds or cashews to just boiled milk or cream, leave to cool, then strain to make a custard-based ice cream.

Roughly chopped sugared almonds with pastel-coloured coatings look good and make easy decorations.

BLANCHING NUTS

1 Put pistachios or almonds into a bowl and just cover with boiling water. Leave to stand for 1–2 minutes until the skins expand and soften.

2 Drain the nuts. With almonds, simply pinch the skins to pop the nuts out. To skin pistachios, rub them together in a dish towel.

TOASTING NUTS

1 For maximum flavour, toast whole or roughly chopped nuts in a dry frying pan on the stove, in a shallow cake tin (pan) under the grill (broiler) or on a baking sheet in a medium oven for 3–4 minutes until golden and lightly roasted. Shake the tin frequently so that the nuts brown evenly.

2 There is no need to add oil, as nuts have such a high natural oil content. You can also toast desiccated (dry, unsweetened) coconut in this way but keep an eye on it; because it is so finely processed, it browns in a matter of seconds.

MAKING PRALINE

1 Gently heat granulated (white) sugar, whole nuts and a little water in a heavy frying pan. Do not use caster (superfine) sugar and do not stir, as this causes the sugar to crystallize, solidify and become opaque.

Continue to heat the sugar, but do not stir the mixture with a spoon. Just tilt the pan gently, if necessary, to mix any sugar that has not dissolved completely.

2 Keep an eye on the nuts, as the sugar and nuts begin to turn golden. Keep the heat low.

3 Pour the praline on to an evenly oiled baking sheet. Then leave to cool and harden. Cover with clear film or put it in a plastic bag. Tap with a rolling pin to break into rough pieces, or grind in a food processor or coffee grinder. Fold into ice cream on the verge of setting.

Layering, rippling and marbling

For a dramatic effect, create different layers of harmonizing ice creams in large or small, rectangular or round moulds. There are plenty of possibilities – just let your imagination take over and enjoy.

HOW TO LAYER ICES
Simple three-tier ice cream

1 When the first flavour has thickened and is semi-frozen, pour it into a 25 x 7.5 x 7.5cm/10 x 3 x 3in terrine or loaf tin (pan) lined with clear film (plastic wrap). Spread it in an even layer and freeze it in the coldest part of the freezer for 1 hour or until firm.

2 Pour in the second layer of semi-frozen ice cream and spread it out evenly. Freeze until firm, add the final ice cream layer and freeze for 4–5 hours until hard. To serve, turn out the ice cream from the mould, peel off the clear film and cut into slices, using a warm knife.

Iced roulade

1 Prepare two quantities of semi-frozen ice cream with flavours that complement each other well. Line a 30 x 23cm/12 x 9in baking sheet with clear film (plastic wrap) or waxed paper. Spread with one quantity of thick, semi-frozen, flavoured ice cream. Freeze for 20 minutes.

2 Spoon the second batch of semi-frozen ice cream over a second piece of clear film or waxed paper to make a rectangle a little smaller than the first. Freeze for 20 minutes. Place this sheet of ice cream over the first layer, then peel off the clear film or waxed paper.

3 Roll the layered ice cream, as if making a Swiss roll, starting from the longest edge and using the clear film or paper to roll it. Pat the ice cream into a neat cylinder, then wrap it in

more clear film. Freeze for several hours, or overnight, until the roll is hard.

4 Peel off the clear film or paper and put the roll on a board. Slice thickly, using a warmed knife.

Chequerboard

1 Make a two-tier terrine, using two of your favourite ice creams layered in a straight-sided 900g/2lb loaf tin (pan) or terrine. Turn out the two-tier terrine on a board and cut it in half lengthways, using a hot knife.

2 Turn one of the halves over to reverse the colour sequence and wrap tightly in clear film to stick them together. Refreeze to harden. To serve, peel away the clear film and slice with a hot knife.

Classic cassata

1 Line a 1.2 litre/2 pint/5 cup bowl with clear film (plastic wrap). Line it with a 2cm/$3/4$in thick layer of semi-frozen strawberry ice cream, using the back of a metal spoon to press the ice cream against the sides and bottom of the bowl. Then cover and freeze for 1–2 hours or until the ice cream lining is firm.

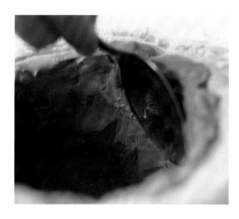

2 Again using the back of a metal spoon, press chocolate ice cream on to the strawberry ice cream in the mould to make a second 2cm/$3/4$in thick layer of chocolate ice cream against the frozen strawberry layer. Leave a space in the centre. Cover and freeze for 1–2 hours more or until the chocolate ice cream is firm.

3 Pack the centre of the mould with tutti frutti ice cream and smooth the top. Cover and freeze the dessert overnight until firm. Dip the mould in hot water for 10 seconds, insert a knife between the clear film and the bowl to loosen the cassata, then invert it on to a serving plate. Lift off the bowl and peel away the clear film (plastic wrap) before decorating the dessert with glacé fruits or chocolate caraque. When ready, serve in wedges.

Individual bombes

1 Line four individual metal moulds with clear film (plastic wrap). Then press a 1cm/$1/2$in layer of dark chocolate ice cream over the bottom and sides of each mould, smoothing the ice cream with the back of a teaspoon. Cover and freeze for 30 minutes or until the ice cream is firm.

2 Add a scoop of vanilla ice cream to the centre of each mould and insert a brandy-soaked prune or cherry into the middle. Smooth the surface, cover and freeze for 4 hours until firm.

3 Dip the filled moulds into a roasting pan filled with hot water for 2 seconds. Invert the moulds on to serving plates and quickly remove the moulds and clear film.

4 Decorate the top and sides of each individual bombe with long sweeping lines of piped white chocolate and serve immediately.

Secrets of success
• Freeze ice cream after each layer has been added so that soft mixtures do not merge together. That way, the finished dessert will have well-defined layers.
• Freeze the mould thoroughly after layering, preferably overnight, so that the layers will not separate when the ice cream is sliced.
• Dip the mould in hot water for 10–15 seconds so that the dessert will turn out easily. Peel off the clear film (plastic wrap) and use a knife dipped into warm water for slicing.

HOW TO RIPPLE ICES

This eye-catching effect is easy to achieve, using ice creams and sauces in contrasting colours.

Make sure flavoured ice creams are too soft to scoop but thick enough to hold their shape. Choose markedly different colours for the most dramatic effect.

Unsweetened strained fruit purées can taste rather icy, so mix them with a thick sugar syrup before swirling with semi-frozen ice cream.

For the easiest rippled ice cream of all, use cold, softly set extra-fruit jam from the jar. Soften firmer jams with a little boiling water before use.

Raspberry ripple

1 Make the vanilla ice cream by hand or churn it in an ice cream maker until it is thick but too soft to scoop.

2 Mix 75g/3oz/6 tbsp caster (superfine) sugar with 60ml/4 tbsp water in a pan. Heat until the sugar dissolves, then boil for 3 minutes until syrupy, but not coloured. Cool slightly. Purée 250g/9oz/1½ cups fresh raspberries in a food processor, then press through a sieve (strainer) over a bowl. Stir in the syrup and chill well.

3 Add alternate spoonfuls of the soft partially frozen vanilla ice cream and the chilled raspberry syrup to a 1 litre/1¾ pint/4 cup plastic tub or similar freezerproof container. Don't worry if the contrasting layers look a little messy to begin with. Stir through the syrup and ice cream two or three times to create a rippled effect. Freeze.

HOW TO MARBLE ICE CREAM

Though similar to the technique used for making a rippled ice cream, marbling creates softer swirls through more thorough mixing. You can use the same combinations of ice cream and syrup as for rippling.

To achieve this effect, marble a chocolate, toffee or fruit sauce through ice cream on the verge of setting. Be careful with toffee sauces as they can dissolve into the ice cream, losing their effect.

1 To achieve the marbling effect, spoon alternate layers of partially frozen ice cream into a freezerproof container, lined with clear film (plastic wrap). With a spoon, drizzle your coloured liquid flavouring, sauce, purée or syrup of choice over each layer.

2 Pass the handle of a wooden spoon through the ice cream and liquid flavouring five or six times to produce a lightly marbled effect. Freeze the ice cream for 4–5 hours or overnight, until firm.

Classic ripple combinations

Mixed berry swirl – strawberry ice cream with raspberry syrup.
Coffee toffee swirl – dark coffee ice cream and rich toffee sauce.
Double chocolate – smooth dark chocolate ice cream rippled with smooth white chocolate ice cream.

Apricot and orange ripple – orange and yogurt ice rippled with apricot sauce.
Creamy toffee ripple – rich toffee sauce and creamy vanilla ice cream.
Raspberry ripple – make your own at home with the very best of ingredients. A timeless classic.

Making biscuits and cones

Stylish and sophisticated, crisp and delicate, biscuits and cones are perfect accompaniments to the smooth texture of ice cream.

BISCUITS
Tuile
SERVES 6

little oil, for greasing
50g/2oz/¹⁄₄ cup unsalted (sweet) butter
75g/3oz/³⁄₄ cup flaked (sliced) almonds
2 medium egg whites
75g/3oz/6 tbsp caster (superfine) sugar
50g/2oz/¹⁄₂ cup plain (all-purpose)
    flour, sifted
rind of ¹⁄₂ orange, finely grated
plus 10ml/2 tsp juice
sifted icing (confectioners') sugar, to decorate

1 Heat the oven to 200°C/400°F/Gas 6. Lightly brush a wooden rolling pin with oil, and line two large baking sheets with baking parchment. Melt the butter in a pan and set it aside. Preheat the grill (broiler). Spread out the flaked almonds on a baking sheet and lightly brown under the grill. Leave to cool, then finely grind half and roughly crush the rest with your fingertips.

2 Put the egg whites and sugar in a bowl and lightly fork them together. Sift in the flour, stir gently to mix, and fold in the melted butter, then the orange rind and juice, and the finely ground nuts.

3 Drop six teaspoons of the mixture, spaced well apart, on to one of the lined baking sheets. Spread the biscuits into thin circles and sprinkle lightly with the crushed nuts. Bake in the oven for 5 minutes until lightly browned around the edges.

4 Loosen one of the biscuits with a metal spatula and drape it over the rolling pin. Shape the remaining biscuits in the same way. Leave for 5 minutes to set while baking a second tray of biscuits. Continue baking and shaping biscuits until all the mixture has been used. Dust with icing sugar and serve with ice cream.

Brandy snaps
MAKES 32

a little oil, for greasing
115g/4oz/¹⁄₂ cup
    unsalted (sweet) butter
115g/4oz/¹⁄₂ cup caster (superfine) sugar
115g/4oz/¹⁄₃ cup golden (light corn) syrup
115g/4oz/1 cup plain (all-purpose) flour
5ml/1 tsp ground ginger
15ml/1 tbsp lemon juice
15ml/1 tbsp brandy

1 Heat the oven to 190°C/375°F/Gas 5. Oil the handles of some wooden spoons. Line two baking sheets with baking parchment. Heat the butter, sugar and syrup in a medium pan, stirring until the butter melts. Take the pan off the heat and sift in the flour and ginger. Mix until smooth. Stir in the lemon juice and brandy.

2 Drop four spaced teaspoons on to the baking sheets. Cook for 5–6 minutes until pale brown and bubbling. Remove from the oven. Leave for 15–30 seconds. Loosen with a metal spatula.

3 Roll each brandy snap around the handle of an oiled wooden spoon and leave, join-side downwards, on a wire rack for 1 minute. Remove the spoon from the first biscuit and repeat.

CONES
Chocolate cones

1 Line the inside of as many cream horn tins as you need with baking parchment so that it sticks out of the ends of the tins slightly and the ends overlap inside.

2 Brush the inside of each cone with melted chocolate, chill for 15 minutes, then brush over a second layer of chocolate. Chill well, then fill with softly set ice cream. Stand the filled cream horn tins in mugs to keep them upright or wedge them in a plastic tub, using crumpled kitchen paper or foil to keep them upright. Freeze until firm.

3 Gently pull the cones out of the tins, holding them by the paper, then carefully peel the paper away. Lay on individual plates and decorate with chocolate curls. Dust each plate with sifted unsweetened cocoa powder.

Tuile ice cream cones

1 Use the basic recipe for tuiles to make ten lacy ice cream cones on wooden moulds. They are extremely fragile, so be careful when filling them. These cones are best eaten on the day that they are made. Make two cones at a time, using 15ml/1 tbsp of mixture per cone. Spread thinly into 10cm/4in circles, sprinkle with nuts and bake at 180°C/350°F/Gas 4 for 5 minutes, until golden around the edges.

2 Have ready an oiled, wooden ice cream cone mould. Loosen a biscuit, using a metal spatula, turn it over and put it on a clean, folded dish towel supported on the palm of your left hand. Lay the cone mould on top and wrap the biscuit around it to form the cone shape. Repeat with the second biscuit, then repeat with the remaining mixture.

Mini cones

1 Using about 10ml/2 tsp of biscuit mixture each time, make two well-spaced mounds on a lined baking sheet. Don't bother to spread them flat. Bake for 4 minutes until the biscuits are starting to brown around the edges.

2 Let the biscuits cool slightly, then loosen with a metal spatula, turn them over and carefully roll them around cream horn tins.

Transform bought cones

1 Liven up ready-made cones by dipping the tops in melted dark, white or milk chocolate and then sprinkling with chopped toasted hazelnuts, toasted flaked (sliced) almonds or roughly chopped pistachio nuts.

2 Coat the rims of cones in melted white chocolate and sprinkle with grated dark chocolate or curls.

3 For children's parties, stud cones with sugar diamonds or sugar flowers, sticking them on with dots of melted white chocolate. Or dip the rims into melted white chocolate, then into pastel-coloured sugar sprinkles.

Making ice cream sauces

No ice cream sundae is complete without one of these popular sauces, which can all be made in advance and refrigerated until needed.

Chocolate sauce

Pour this delicious sauce, hot or cold, over vanilla, milk chocolate ice cream or ice cream sundaes.

MAKES 400ML/14FL OZ/1²/₃ CUPS

25g/1oz/2 tbsp butter
25g/1oz/2 tbsp caster (superfine) sugar
30ml/2 tbsp golden (light corn) syrup
200g/7oz luxury plain (unsweetened)
    cooking chocolate
150ml/¹/₄ pint/²/₃ cup
semi-skimmed (low-fat) milk
45ml/3 tbsp double (heavy) cream

1 In a pan, mix the butter, caster sugar, syrup and the chocolate broken into pieces. Heat very gently, stirring occasionally, until the chocolate melts.

2 Gradually stir in the milk and cream and bring just to the boil, stirring until smooth. Serve hot or cold.

Butterscotch sauce

This creamy toffee sauce is delicious, warm or cool, with vanilla, coffee or yogurt ice creams.

MAKES 475ML/16FL OZ/2 CUPS

200g/7oz/1 cup caster (superfine) sugar
45ml/3 tbsp each
cold water and
boiling water
75g/3oz/6 tbsp unsalted (sweet) butter
150ml/¹/₄ pint/²/₃ cup double
    (heavy) cream

1 Gently heat the sugar and 45ml/3 tbsp cold water in a pan, without stirring, until all the sugar has dissolved.

2 Bring to the boil and boil until the sugar starts to turn golden. Quickly take the pan off the heat and immediately plunge the base into cold water to prevent the sugar from overbrowning.

3 Standing as far back as possible, and protecting your hand with an oven glove, add the 45ml/3 tbsp boiling water to the caramel mixture, which will splutter and spit. Add the butter and tilt the pan to mix the ingredients together. Leave to cool for 5 minutes.

4 Gradually stir in the cream, mix well and pour into a jug.

Melba sauce

Of all the classic ice cream sauces, this is perhaps the best known of all. It is perfect with scoops of vanilla ice cream and sliced ripe peaches. Some versions use cornflour (cornstarch) but this simple recipe is best.

MAKES 200ML/7FL OZ/SCANT 1 CUP

250g/9oz/1¹/₃ cups fresh or thawed
    frozen raspberries
30ml/2 tbsp icing (confectioners') sugar

1 Purée the raspberries in a food processor or blender until smooth. Pour into a sieve (strainer) set over a bowl and press through, discarding the seeds. Sift in the icing sugar, mix well and chill until required.

Making decorations

Complete the simplest dish of beautifully scooped ice cream or a party-style sundae with one of these professional decorations and you can't fail to impress your dinner guests.

Dark chocolate caraque

1 With a metal spatula or the back of a spoon, spread melted dark (bittersweet) chocolate over a marble slab, cheese board or an offcut of kitchen work surface, to a depth of about 5mm/¼ in. Leave in a cool place to set.

2 Draw a long, fine-bladed cook's knife across the chocolate at a 45° angle, using a see-saw action to pare away long curls. If the chocolate is too soft, put it in the fridge for 5 minutes or in a cold place for 15 minutes. Do not overchill.

Piped chocolate shapes

Spoon a little melted dark (bittersweet) chocolate into a paper piping bag and snip off the tip. Pipe squiggly shapes, stars, hearts, butterflies, etc on to a lined baking sheet. Peel off when cool and chill until required.

Chocolate rose leaves

Brush melted dark chocolate very evenly over the underside of clean, dry rose leaves. Avoid brushing over the edges. Put the leaf on to a non-stick parchment-lined baking sheet and leave in a cool place to set. Carefully peel each leaf away and chill until required.

Two-tone caraque

1 Spoon alternate lines of melted white and dark chocolate over a marble slab or cheese board, or an offcut of work surface and spread lightly so that all the chocolate is the same height. Leave to cool and harden.

2 Pare away long, thin curls of chocolate with a fine-bladed cook's knife in the same way that you do when making dark chocolate caraque.

Simple chocolate curls

Holding a bar of dark, white or milk chocolate over a plate, pare curls away from the edge of the bar, using a vegetable peeler. Lift the pared curls carefully with a flat blade or a metal spatula and arrange as you desire.

Chocolate-dipped fruits

Choose from tiny strawberries (still with their green hulls attached), tiny clusters of green or red grapes, physalis or cherries, with their stalks. It can also look very effective if you dip half the fruits in dark chocolate and the remainder in white chocolate. Leave the fruits to set on a baking sheet lined with baking parchment or foil.

Caramel shapes

Caramel is also suitable for making fancy shapes to decorate ice cream sundaes. Drizzle shapes such as treble clefs, graduated zig-zags, spirals, curly scribbles, initials, musical notes, stars or hearts on to a lightly oiled baking sheet. Vary the sizes from small decorations about 5cm/2in to larger 10cm/4in-long shapes.

Caramel-dipped fruits

Half-dip peeled physalis, whole strawberries or cherries (with the stalks intact) into the warm syrup, then leave to cool and harden on an oiled baking sheet.

Coloured chocolate

1 Pipe random lines of melted dark (bittersweet) chocolate over a piece of baking parchment. Overpipe with piped white chocolate. Using pink liquid food colouring, tint a little of the melted white chocolate.

2 Pipe a third layer of chocolate squiggles, in pink, over the dark and white layers. Chill until set.

3 Break the coloured shapes into jagged fragments of varying sizes and stick them into ice cream to decorate. They look particularly good on top of ice cream sundaes.

Decorating with exotic fruits
You can effortlessly transform simple ice cream dishes into a gourmet feast with the addition of a few pretty exotic fruits. Physalis look marvellous with their papery cases twisted back to reveal the berry fruit, while pearly white lychees add a dramatic note if the red skin is torn off into a spiral. Or you could try using a quartered fig, with its delicate ruby flesh, or a few jewel-like pomegranate seeds or perfumed passion fruit seeds.

Frosted flowers

1 Brush lightly beaten egg white over edible flowers (see page 206).

2 Sprinkle with caster (superfine) sugar and leave to dry on a plate. Always use on the day of making.

Citrus curls

1 Pare the coloured rind only of an orange, lemon or lime.

2 Dust the citrus curls with caster sugar and then sprinkle them over citrus-based ices such as lemon sorbet.

Citrus corkscrews

1 Pare long, very narrow strips of orange, lemon or lime rind.

2 Twist them tightly around cocktail sticks. Slide the sticks out and hang the curls over the edge of dishes.

Meringue dainties

1 Mix 2 egg whites and 115g/4oz/½ cup caster sugar. Spoon into a large piping bag with either a small plain 5mm/¼ in or a 9mm/³/8 in nozzle.

2 Pipe heart shapes, zigzags, shooting stars, geometric shapes, flowers, etc on to baking sheets lined with baking parchment.

3 Sprinkle with caster sugar and bake at low heat until firm enough to lift off the paper easily. Cool, then store in a cake tin for up to 1 week.

Index